ANTI-SEMITISM BEFORE THE HOLOCAUST

Anti-Semitism before the Holocaust

ALBERT S. LINDEMANN

An imprint of **Pearson Education**

Harlow, England · London · New York · Reading, Massachusetts · San Francisco
Toronto · Don Mills, Ontario · Sydney · Tokyo · Singapore · Hong Kong · Seoul
Taipei · Cape Town · Madrid · Mexico City · Amsterdam · Munich · Paris · Milan

Pearson Education Limited
Edinburgh Gate
Harlow
Essex CM20 2JE
England

and Associated Companies throughout the world.

Visit us on the World Wide Web at:
www.pearsoned.co.uk

First published 2000

ISBN 978-0-582-36964-1

British Library Cataloguing-in-Publication Data
A catalogue record for this book is available from the British Library

Library of Congress Cataloging-in-Publication Data
Lindemann, Albert S.
    Anti-semitism before the Holocaust / Albert Lindemann.
        p. cm. -- (Seminar studies in history)
    Includes bibliographical references and index.
    ISBN 0-582-36964-9 (pbk.)
    1. Antisemitism--History. I. Title: Antisemitism before the Holocaust. II. Title. III.
Series.

DS145 .L585 2000
305.892'4--dc21   99.047311

10   9   8   7   6   5
09 08 07

Set by 7 in 10/12 Sabon
Printed in Malaysia, LSP

Dedicated to Grace Enola, in deep admiration and love

CONTENTS

AN INTRODUCTION TO THE SERIES

Such is the pace of historical enquiry in the modern world that there is an ever-widening gap between the specialist article or monograph, incorporating the results of current research, and general surveys, which inevitably become out of date. *Seminar Studies in History* are designed to bridge this gap. The series was founded by Patrick Richardson in 1966 and his aim was to cover major themes in British, European and World history. Between 1980 and 1996 Roger Lockyer continued his work, before handing the editorship over to Clive Emsley and Gordon Martel. Clive Emsley is Professor of History at the Open University, while Gordon Martel is Professor of International History at the University of Northern British Columbia, Canada and Senior Research Fellow at De Montfort University.

All the books are written by experts in their field who are not only familiar with the latest research but have often contributed to it. They are frequently revised, in order to take account of new information and interpretations. They provide a selection of documents to illustrate major themes and provoke discussion, and also a guide to further reading. The aim of *Seminar Studies* is to clarify complex issues without over-simplifying them, and to stimulate readers into deepening their knowledge and understanding of major themes and topics.

NOTE ON REFERENCING SYSTEM

Readers should note that numbers in square brackets [5] refer them to the corresponding entry in the Bibliography at the end of the book (specific page numbers are given in italics). A number in square brackets preceded by *Doc.* [*Doc. 5*] refers readers to the corresponding item in the Documents section which follows the main text.

AUTHOR'S ACKNOWLEDGEMENTS

First thanks must go to my wife, Barbara, who is always the first to read my drafts and is usually my most perceptive critic, both as to style and content. That she has good-naturedly put up with these impositions – and seemingly endless revisions – for over thirty-five years is but one small indication of how lucky I have been in love.

This book derives to an important degree from my articles and books over the past ten to fifteen years. Since I began to teach and do research on the history of anti-Semitism, nearly twenty years ago, my colleagues at the University of California, Santa Barbara have been invaluable in their supportive yet rigorous readings of my work. Scholars at a number of other universities, too, have offered me support and valuable criticism. I will not repeat the many names already listed in my previous books, but I do feel the need to thank those scholars, at my university and others, with whom I have been in recent personal contact and who have helped in significant ways since the publication of my last book: Harold Marcuse, William Rubinstein, John Murray Cuddihy, Steven Beller, Robert Skloot and Kevin MacDonald.

I must single out Richard S. Levy, Professor of History at the University of Illinois at Chicago and moderator of H-ANTI-SEMITISM, for special thanks. He gave particularly careful readings to the manuscript drafts of this book and my previous one, *Esau's Tears*. Beyond that, I have relied on his wide knowledge and expert advice concerning a large number of scholarly topics – offered, I should say, with tact and wonderful wit. It would be difficult for me to imagine a better model of a scholar than he.

Much of the material in these pages has been tested in lectures and classroom discussions at the University of California at Santa Barbara. Similarly, chapter drafts of my books have been read by my students, both undergraduate and graduate; our sometimes passionate exploration of issues of ethnic/religious identity and hostility has been extremely valuable to me. In complete sincerity I can say that I have often learned more from them than I have taught. I have also carried on an active correspondence with graduate students from other universities, and one in particular, Patrick O'Brien, read draft chapters and offered valuable comments, for which I am sincerely grateful.

Finally, warm thanks to the series editor, Gordon Martel, to copy-editor, Sarah Bury, and to house editor, Verina Pettigrew, and commissioning editor, Emma Mitchell. It has been a pleasure to work with editors so patient, gracious, and professional.

ASL
October, 1999
Santa Barbara, Calif.

PUBLISHER'S ACKNOWLEDGEMENTS

We are indebted to the National Council of the Churches of Christ in the USA for permission to reproduce scripture quotations from the *Revised Standard Version of The Bible,* copyright 1946, 1952, and 1971 by the Division of Christian Education of the National Council of the Churches of Christ in the USA. All rights reserved.

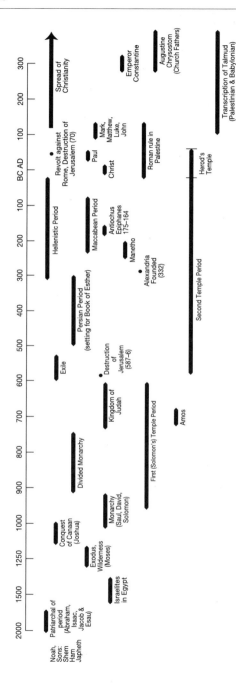

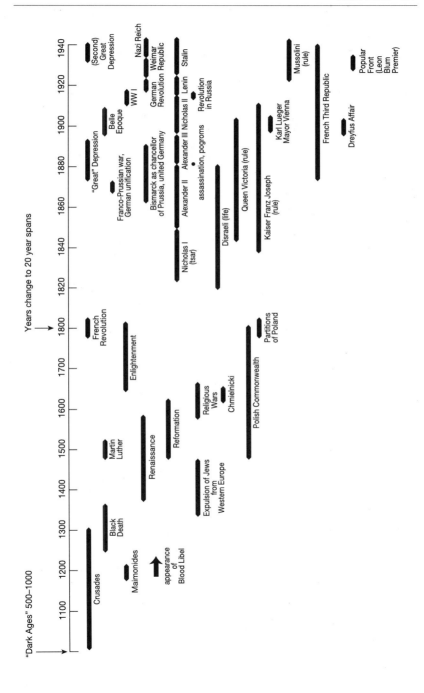

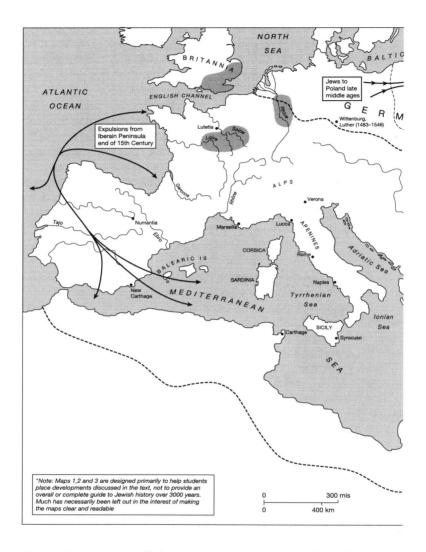

Map 1   Europe and the Mediterranean from ancient times to the end of the

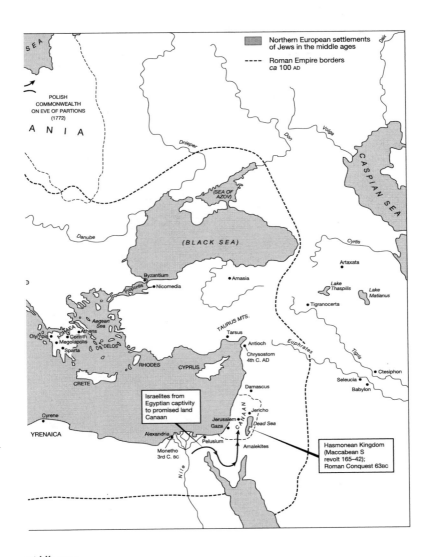

middle ages

Map 2   Late nineteenth and early twentieth century Europe

FINLAND

L. Onega

L. Ladoga

R. Dvina

St. Petersburg

Kazan

URAL MOUNTAINS

R. Volga

Moscow

R. Oka

R U S S I A

R. Ural

Riga

BALTIC PROVINCES

Memel

Tambov

Minsk

Voronezh

Major battlefields 1914–20 (and major areas of Jewish settlement)

R. Pripet

Warsaw

R. Volga

Lodz

Brest-Litovsk

Kiev

R. Dnieper

R. Don

Krakow

R. Dniester

R. Bug

UKRAINIA

Rostov

Budapest

BESSARABIA

CASPIAN SEA

HUNGARY

Odessa

SEA OF AZOV

Petrovsk

RUMANIA

CRIMEA

GEORGIA

Baku

Bucharest

DOBRUDJA

BLACK SEA

Batum

Tbilisi

Belgrade

R. Danube

Erzerum

PERSIA

MONTE NEGRO

BULGARIA

Sofia

Constantinople

SERBIA

Angora

R. Tigris

ALBANIA

Mosul

GREECE

AEGEAN SEA

OTTOMAN EMPIRE

IONIAN ISLANDS

Smyrna

Aleppo

R. Euphrates

Baghdad

RHODES

Nicosia

CYPRUS

CRETE

ARABIA

Damascus

SEA

British Palestine Mandate 1920–48

Jerusalem

Bengazi

Alexandria

ITANIA

EGYPT

R. Nile

Cairo

0   300 km

0   400 km

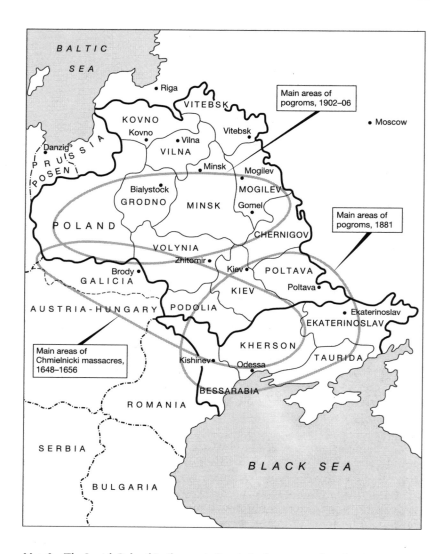

*Map 3   The Jewish Pale of Settlement in Russia in the nineteenth and early twentieth
centuries*

INTRODUCTION: THEMES, GOALS, PROBLEMS

UNDERSTANDING ANTI-SEMITISM – IS IT POSSIBLE?

Some time ago a graduate student I know remarked that when she was younger the history of anti-Semitism was like sex education: 'No one taught it formally, all the students knew something about it anyway, but the information we acquired was generally garbled and incomplete.'[1] Some years before that, my seven-year-old son asked me, 'Why do people hate the Jews?' He had several Jewish playmates, had been to their homes, and had met their parents. 'They're so nice ... ,' he added, genuinely puzzled.

My son's question and the graduate student's remark have served as incentives and reference points for me in composing this volume.[2] The situation referred to by the graduate student has changed in some important regards but has not greatly improved, particularly in terms of the availability of short histories that also meet scholarly standards. A large number of books have appeared about the topic of Jew-hatred – too many, one sometimes hears – but most of those addressing a wide public lack interpretive ambition and scope; they tend, as does popular history on a range of topics, toward vivid description rather than rigorous and balanced analysis. Our emotions are engaged with horrifying narratives but our intellects are left dissatisfied – *why* have these things happened? Moreover, most of the books devoted to the history of Jew-hatred are very long; many of the best cover only limited areas and are read mostly by scholars. Here, as in so many areas of modern life, there remains a lamentable gap between what

---

1 In a post by Jo Miller, Mon., 9 Feb 1998 11:20:0500, to **H-ANTISEMITISM@ MSU.EDU**
2 To an important degree these pages represent an effort to condense and make more approachable the contents of two previous books I have written on anti-Semitism: *The Jew Accused: Three Anti-Semitic Affairs* (1991) [107] and *Esau's Tears: Modern Anti-Semitism and the Rise of the Jews* (1997) [108].

scholarly experts write for one another and what the general public reads or otherwise knows about.

Given the dizzying complexity of the subject of Jew-hatred throughout history and the extent to which often blinding emotions are engaged by discussions of it, one might well conclude that any attempt to write an account that is both brief and critical of much existing literature would be hazardous if not foolhardy; the un-avoidable omissions and condensations will disappoint if not offend many readers; misunderstandings are almost inevitable. Such con-siderations have haunted me in composing nearly every line of this work. But I have concluded that the effort is worthwhile, in spite of its many risks, indeed partly because of them, since the hazards of the field have caused many authors to shy away from it and have worked to limit the openness as well as the interpretive ambition of existing works on anti-Semitism.

Hollywood and television have recently devoted much attention to the Holocaust and to Nazism. The attention has its full share of problems, even for the short period from World War I to the end of World War II, but one special problem is that the deeper roots of Nazi Jew-hatred are typically neglected or presented in a ham-fisted form. Museums devoted to the mass murder of Europe's Jews have sprung up in many locations; the Holocaust Museum in Washington, D.C., has won widespread and for the most part well-deserved praise. Whatever the pros and cons of this recent burst of attention – what some have derided as 'Holocaustomania' – one must ask whether it has contributed to a better understanding of Jew-hatred. More is not necessarily better, nor is loud always more effective than mild. I believe that this attention, by an almost exclusive concern with negative themes, has made more problematic both Jewish self-under-standing and an understanding of Jews by non-Jews. Similarly, it has encumbered our understanding of Jew-hatred by simplifying its nature, often to the point of caricature.

An occurrence so monstrous as the Holocaust stuns and disorients. Studies devoted to it range across a remarkable interpretive spectrum. At one end, there are those who claim that the sheer horror of that mass murder can never and *should never* be absorbed. More pre-cisely, they believe that efforts to understand, even if well intentioned, inevitably lose touch with the unspeakable suffering of the Holo-caust's victims, becoming abstract, academic, and remote. Holocaust survivors in particular tend to resent the theorizing of those who were not there. Lawrence Langer argues that efforts to learn lessons about the Holocaust are misconceived, finally futile; nothing of a redemptive value can be salvaged from the ineffable tragedy [99]. The acclaimed film-maker Claude Lanzmann (producer of the film *Shoah*) has gone so far as to insist that attempts to understand the perpetrators, the Nazis and their allies in various countries, by an open-minded examination of context and motive, become 'obscene,' since they open the door to sympathy for mass murderers. A bit too threatening for him is the old French adage, *tout comprendre, c'est tout pardonner* (to understand everything is to pardon everything) [145 *pp. 252–3*].

At the other end of the interpretive spectrum, many scholars maintain that the Holocaust was perpetrated by human beings and can be understood by human beings, at least as much as other horrors in history can be understood; there is nothing so utterly 'unique' about the Holocaust, nothing about the suffering in it that is so completely unprecedented and horrific that it somehow stands out- side history and is beyond human comprehension. Indeed, many believe that comprehension is essential, a pressing moral obligation; we *must* study this event, 'learn lessons,' in order to prevent some- thing like it from occurring in the future.

Given these gaping differences, it should come as no surprise that major interpreters of the Holocaust – survivors, scholars, journalists, novelists, movie-makers – have repeatedly engaged in ugly clashes. A comparable unpleasantness among interpreters in the long-range history of anti-Semitism has not arisen, but a kindred dogmatism is nonetheless there, as is a tendency toward mysticism. A number of observers, for example, have suggested that anti-Semitism throughout history must be considered fundamentally incomprehensible and that efforts to understand Jew-haters run the risk of seeming to provide excuses for them [108 *p. 531 ff*].

One finds in many histories an abundant and indignant description of anti-Semitic theories, agitators, and events, accompanied by remarkably reticent or feeble efforts to explain what provoked them. In short, ostensibly the same concern: somehow the shock and sting will be lost by 'too much' understanding. Implicitly at least, these observers maintain that the irreducible mystery must remain; historical analysis must not be allowed to weaken moral outrage.

We come to a fundamental question: how does one conceptualize evil, which is itself considered dark, mysterious and endlessly elusive? Might it be suggested that anti-Semites, if themselves poor and oppressed – as many certainly were – deserve at least some kind of 'sympathetic' understanding for their own victimhood, in the sense of an imaginative leap in the direction of recognizing how they were striking out against Jews in often blind anger? The hatreds and frustrations of the poor and oppressed, as well as their cruelties, are the stuff of history. It seems an odd conclusion that only in the case of hatred against Jews we should shun efforts to understand those emotions.

Even when anti-Semites were rich, privileged, and highly educated, as they also often were, we might wonder if it should be taboo to ask, 'might I have entertained similar ideas?' Is uncompromising moral condemnation – a dogmatic refusal to 'understand' – the most effective way to remedy anti-Semitism? One might easily conclude that such mental and moral inflexibility often makes things worse.

In a related way, how much should an account of Jew-hatred concern itself with an analysis of the inner life and activities of Jews themselves? Are they to be conceived as actors in this story, 'fighting back,' yet inevitably revealing their own kinds of frailties, moral failures, and degrees of responsibility? Or is the only proper attitude one that portrays them as passive and thus wholly innocent victims?

At any rate, a key point must not be missed: for most of the history of Europe and America, Jews and non-Jews have not been anything like equals in terms of power. How does one fairly evaluate the historical role of the relatively powerless in relation to the powerful? As a start, we can say that it is anything but easy.

ETERNAL ANTI-SEMITISM AND 'BLAMING THE JEWS'

Expressions of hatred for Jews have emerged time and again in remarkably different kinds of cultures, over thousands of years. Some authors have argued that the explanation for that 'longest hatred' is perfectly obvious, and indeed that the hatred is not at all mysterious. It lies in certain qualities of Jews and Judaism, qualities that understandably have provoked hostility on the part of those among whom Jews have lived. The real historical puzzle, then, is not that Jews have been hated, given their enduring qualities, but that they have survived at all. Arthur Koestler,[3] the noted Jewish author, put the matter bluntly: 'The Jewish religion, unlike any other, is racially discriminatory, nationally segregative, and socially tension-creating' [*93 p. 111*]. Three hundred years earlier, the celebrated Jewish philosopher, Baruch Spinoza, made similar observations. Hatred of Jews throughout history has been the result of their peculiar kind of separatism, itself related to their sense of superiority to others. The themes of

---

3   Further biographical information, such as birth and death dates, on historical figures mentioned in the text is included in the Glossary and Cast of Characters, as are definitions of terms that some readers may need to have more amply identified.

their religion, particularly those that denigrate other beliefs and customs, have made them hated [129].

Many have objected that accounting for anti-Semitism in that way is unacceptable because it involves 'blaming the victim;' anti-Semitism is not a Jewish problem, not even a mutual problem of Jews and non-Jews, but uniquely a non-Jewish problem [186]. Replies to that objection have been no less combative. Can one really believe that in every instance, over hundreds and thousands of years, hostility to Jews has been always exclusively the result of moral flaws in non-Jews and never in the Jews themselves? Even granting that Jews have usually lacked power, can their activities, individually or collectively, have been so consistently above reproach, never the 'real' source of friction?

The Nazi experience no doubt accounts for much of the passion and intransigence with which those arguments have been presented. To suggest that the Jews and the Nazis somehow shared responsibility – even to the slightest degree – for Nazi hatred comes across as absurd and repellent. But can we let this extreme case serve as an adequate model for all of history? Can the Arab–Israeli conflict be conceptualized as the exclusive fault of the Arabs, rather than a tragic struggle of two historically victimized peoples with conflicting claims? It is difficult to avoid the conclusion that here as very often a desire for a genuine understanding of group conflict in history plays a smaller role than anger and resentment, linked to the tendency of various constituencies to embrace victimhood for the benefits and immunities that victims are believed to enjoy by right.

'Eternal' anti-Semitism, at any rate, has often been exaggerated. Jews have in fact not encountered hostility everywhere they have settled, at least not by a majority of the people. Ruling elites as well as common people have time and again found at least part of the Jewish population to be useful, even admirable. For such reasons those in power have often defended Jews against the anger of unruly mobs or other criminally violent groups that have been attracted to plunder when Jews are perceived as weak or vulnerable.

One needs also to realize that those 'certain qualities' that are said to characterize Jews can be understood in both negative and positive ways. Jews have been portrayed as perennially battling for truth, justice, and conscience based on their belief in a single true god and his law – a sure formula for being resented by that part of the population throughout history that has thrived on falsehood, injustice, and immorality. Yet even those who have admired the Jews as upholders of morality have also typically described them as an 'irritating' or 'disturbing' element of the population, often prone to exaggerated, irresponsible, or dangerously doctrinaire positions. A common remark in modern times has been that Jews in non-Jewish society are like leavening in bread or salt in food, useful or pleasant in small amounts but unpleasant and even destructive when too abundant or, in a common and pregnant phrase, 'out of control.' One can see, then, how such language could evolve into language that speaks of the Jews as germs or cancer.

This compound image of Jews – critical outsiders, useful but also potentially destructive – has been amply acknowledged by quite different kinds of observers over the centuries. Sigmund Freud, the founder of psychoanalysis, candidly described himself as a detached and ironic observer, in his words a 'godless Jew', helping people to come to grips with excruciatingly unwelcome truths about themselves – and earning himself detestation as well as admiration for that role. The Jewish revolutionary, Leon Trotsky, believed he was bringing secular salvation to the world through Communist dictatorship, incurring even more violent and widespread hatred if also acclaim and even veneration in some quarters.

The non-Jewish and arch-conservative, T. S. Eliot, winner of the Nobel Prize for Literature in 1948, asserted that 'too many freethinking Jews' are undesirable in any 'well-ordered society.' He found ready agreement on that point from the American hero, Charles Lindbergh: 'A few Jews add strength and character to a country, but too many create chaos' [16 *p. 586*]. Adolf Hitler asserted that Jews of any sort and in any numbers were ultimately ruinous to non-Jewish peoples. Theodore Herzl, a founding figure of modern Jewish nationalism, or Zionism, concluded that, given their nature, Jews would inevitably be hated by non-Jews, once Jewish numbers and influence began to grow – 'too much' [108 *p. 321*; 135].

These colorful remarks can, however, give a mistaken impression. A much neglected point about Jew-hatred is that many people throughout history have felt neither pronounced hate nor love for Jews. Many, perhaps most non-Jews in Europe and America have been indifferent to or moved by relatively mild opinions about Jews, in part because of their lack of contact with them; Jews simply did not enter their lives to a significant degree. Carefully exploring the wide spectrum, from the fringe that actively hates through the large mass of mostly indifferent, to the fringe that admires, is revealing. Such a task, however, is considered to be misconceived by those who passionately insist that hostility to Jews has been both pervasive and intense through-out history. Many of them also argue that hatred of Jews always has been 'essentially the same,' akin to cancer in that even the smallest amounts of it must be seen as cause for grave concern, given its peculiar proclivity to spread suddenly and unpredictably, destroying its host. (There is a remarkable parallel in the use of cancer or disease imagery by anti-Semites and their most inflamed opponents.)

The following pages will point to the evidence that hatred of Jews, rather than being a single entity with constant traits, is multidimensional; it has changed both in quality and intensity over the centuries, varying substantially from region to region. Pre-Christian hostility to Jews was significantly different from that of the Christian era, but even within the history of Christianity there have long been contrasting images as well as important transformations in the way that Jews have been conceptualized. And in modern times, with the advent of secular universalism and 'scientific' racism, there have been yet other fundamental shifts in attitudes to Jews. To be sure, a case can be made for a kind of sameness in the charges made against Jews (for example, their arrogance and contempt for others, their outsider's destructiveness of the societies within which they live), but that sameness is only of the vaguest and most general nature, with decidedly variable implications in terms of anti-Jewish action, as we will see.

JEWISH AND NON-JEWISH PERSPECTIVES

The graduate student mentioned in the opening paragraph is not Jewish, and the situation about which she complained (sex and Jew-hatred both being taboo topics) referred primarily to non-Jews. For Jews, the situation is usually different, in that most of them come into contact with more information about Jew-hatred in history than non-Jews do. Indeed, a belief in the lasting hostility of non-Jews or the Other Nations (*goyim* in Hebrew) can be described as a key tenet of Jewish religious and cultural traditions, prominently seen in the narratives associated with such holidays as Passover, Hanukkah, or Purim. A belief that Jews have always faced a tenacious and mysterious hostility has been passed down from generation to generation, surviving even among Jews who have little to do with Judaism and who are mostly ignorant of Jewish history. The underlying message – 'we have always been hated' – may be understood as a mirror image of the belief by anti-Semites that Jews 'always' hate other peoples and religions.

The history of the relations of Jews and the Other Nations is explosive in part because it can be so threatening; the way in which it is composed can make both non-Jews and Jews uncomfortable, if not indignant, though usually in very different ways. In the modern American context, ranging from the Christian churches to the Ivy League colleges, there has been, until quite recently, a silence, a reticence on the non-Jewish side to come to terms with a disturbing history of prejudice and exclusion. In Europe, of course, the record has been one of violence and mass murder, with an even more striking disinclination on the part of some Europeans to face forthrightly what happened to their Jewish neighbors and fellow citizens in the 1930s and 1940s.

Jews and Jewish institutions, and of course Jewish scholars, have been less hesitant to grapple with that painful and threatening history. For many years it has been overwhelmingly Jewish rather than non-Jewish scholars who have written about anti-Semitism. Indeed, one sometimes hears the complaint that Jews tend to be obsessive about the subject; some are dogmatic and bullying in discussions of it, while others use it in a manipulative way in their relations to non-Jews. Non-Jews, on the other hand, are criticized by Jews for making uninformed and wounding comments, or indeed for thinking that the subject should just be dropped, allowed to fade into a well-deserved oblivion. But it is a topic that will not go away.

DEFINING ANTI-SEMITISM

Efforts to define anti-Semitism have been so numerous and inconclusive as to invite ridicule. The term itself is relatively new, dating to the 1870s. It came into use at that time to describe hostility to the Jewish or Semitic race, posing as a 'scientific' issue, as distinguished from earlier 'superstitious' or religious hatred. But the term was used confusedly and inconsistently from the beginning. Moreover, defining what was meant by the Jewish race was no less fraught with difficulties than defining what it meant to be a Jew in a religious sense.

To be sure, traditional Jewish religious law (*halakha*) offers what may seem an unequivocal definition of being a Jew: having a Jewish mother or having converted to Judaism according to a traditional ceremony, involving circumcision and a ritual bath among other things. But once Jews by the millions began to distance themselves from traditional Judaism in the nineteenth century that definition satisfied fewer and fewer of them. In part for such reasons, Jews themselves were for some years attracted to racial definitions of Jewishness or 'Semitism.' A non-religious Jew, for example, would identify himself as a Jew or Semite 'by race but not religion.' The notion of a Jewish race, by the late twentieth century no longer accepted by most educated observers as useful, was widely embraced in the nineteenth and early twentieth centuries, especially by the educated.

To have been consistent to the etymology of the term, anti-Semitism should have referred only to racial hatred, but it almost immediately became used in a blurred, more generic way, and that broader usage has survived to this day. The tendency to confuse racial essence and religious belief in the late nineteenth century was related to the fact that being Jewish was, and indeed remains, itself a mingled and elusive matter. It is both religious and cultural; one might even say that it retains a 'racial' aspect, in the sense that Jewishness has an element of identity by descent. A person with Jewish parents remains Jewish – both in the eyes of traditional Jews and anti-Semites – even when no longer accepting Judaic beliefs.

Other terms have been used, both before and after 'anti-Semitism' was coined, such as 'Judeophobia' or simply 'Jew-hatred,' but they have not replaced the ambiguous, confusing but still widely used term anti-Semitism. Judeophobia suggests an interesting nuance in conceptualization: the 'anti' of anti-Semitism indicates opposition or hatred, while 'phobia' suggests that fear and aversion are mixed with hatred. Most modern anti-Semites have in fact both feared and hated Jews.

Despite a growing conviction in the nineteenth century that character was determined by race, by no means everyone accepted that belief. Even among those who did, not all concluded that the Semitic race was inferior or destructive. Revealingly, among those who did perceive a distasteful quality to 'Semitism' were many Jews themselves; both Jews and non-Jews in the nineteenth century typically believed, especially in western and central Europe, that Jews needed to 'improve' themselves, casting off 'ghetto traits' (servility, deviousness, clannishness), although how much those traits ultimately derived from race as contrasted to environment was often hotly contested. Many Jews felt ineffable mixtures of inferiority and superiority, especially in a moral or intellectual sense. Sometimes their assertions of superiority were a transparent defense mechanism, but such assertions also derived from deeply rooted cultural and religious traditions, to say nothing of the fact that in a number of regards (e.g., literacy) Jews were often measurably superior to those among whom they lived.

A central issue in arriving at a useful and coherent definition of anti-Semitism is whether any and all forms of hostility, ranging from mere irritation to raging hatred, are properly considered anti-Semitic.

Many scholars have urged that the term be reserved for the more pronounced and irrational forms of hostility, especially those that look to concerted legal action against Jews. Such indeed was the intent of many anti-Semites when the term was first coined. Jewish folk humor has put the matter of the irrational content in a typically self-mocking form: 'Anti-Semitism is hating Jews more than they deserve to be hated.' That leaves open the hardly surprising possibility that Jews have sometimes deserved hatred, individually or in more general ways. It also suggests that the most rigorous and useful definition of anti-Semitism points to an essential element of irrationality: anti-Semitic hostilities can only partially be explained by tangible issues (sometimes called 'reality-based' hatred); the more extreme forms derive in significant part from fantasies or myths about Jews, particularly those that evoke revulsion, dread, or panic.

We all recognize that hostility can arise from clear and direct causes: 'I hate Moishe Cohen because he cheated me.' Hatred can also arise from causes cloaked in murky symbolism and mystery, 'beyond logic,' reflecting deeper yearnings, tribal loyalties, or more perversely malevolent kinds of consciousness: 'I hate all Jews because they killed Christ and hate His followers.' However, most antipathies represent impenetrable mixtures of irrational and more comprehensible hostility: 'I hate Moishe Cohen, a typically devious and destructive Jew, who cheated me.'

To summarize, then, anti-Semitism is most usefully conceptualized as hatred/fear of Jews that includes a key element of irrationality or emotionally fraught fantasy. But that fantasy is typically intertwined with elements of more accurate or concrete perceptions. It is obviously not a fantasy to say that Jews reject Christ as well as peculiarly Christian messages of universal redemption. Such perfectly accurate observations, it might be noted, provide us already with enough to explain the sometimes raging hostilities of the two groups. Christian sects have murdered one another by the thousands for less. But the further step of asserting that all Jews hate all Christians (or vice versa) is unwarranted by the evidence. To push the matter to a logical and revealing extreme, it is a complete fantasy to say that Jews kill Christian children for their blood to use in matzos at Passover [100 *p. 11 ff*].

This 'Blood Libel' is a good example of a fantasy that has served as ostensible motive for brutal outbreaks of violence against Jews. That fantasy took on a life of its own, passed down from generation to generation, without reinforcement from reality. (No credible evidence has ever been produced that Jews, even wayward sects of them, have ever killed Christian children for their blood.) On the other hand, charges that Jews have been devious merchants or exploitative money-lenders have been linked to the fact that in many areas and periods disproportionate numbers of Jews were merchants or money-lenders; by mere human probability one can conclude that at least some of them did not observe the highest moral standards.

Abstract definitions have their uses, but they should be considered only a beginning. The historian's approach emphasizes that to understand what anti-Semitism is one needs to confront abstract definitions with concrete evidence of what hatred of Jews has been in history. A related issue is where the historian's gaze should concentrate. Is the history of anti-Semitism to be primarily the history of ideas? And what is the power of ideas as contrasted with the power of material forces? How do we conceptualize the role of 'great men,' or powerful historical actors?

My answers to these questions will take shape in the following chapters, but at this point let me observe that I have attempted to blend or synthesize various approaches. In particular, I have tried to understand the way that fantasy (ideologies, myths and other less formal productions of the mind) and reality (developments in the material world) interact. I have also attempted to conceptualize the interplay of Jew and non-Jew as one of active if usually unequal agents.

There is overwhelming evidence that anti-Semitism flares up in times of trouble (depressions, wars, epidemics), and so those times need to be given special consideration. There is also persuasive evidence that individuals have made a decisive difference in history – 'no Hitler no Holocaust' – and so I will pay special attention to the peculiar characters as well as the ideas of a number of major historical actors. Finally, there is evidence that periods of rising Jew-hatred throughout history are related to periods of rapid Jewish rise (in numbers, wealth, social and political position). Such was especially the case in modern times, when the rise of the Jews may well have been more substantial and more dramatic than in any previous period of Jewish history.

Another revealing way to conceptualize anti-Semitism is to state that the anti-Semite believes that Jews are an evil influence in the world, whereas a philo-Semite sees Jewish presence as beneficial. A rise of the Jews will obviously be perceived in quite different ways by either group. It is also obvious that most non-Jews do not fit neatly into one or the other category. The Christian has almost by definition an ambiguous and conflicted evaluation of the Jewish role in the history of Christianity, with significant variations among the many

Christian denominations. But for nearly all kinds of Christians a sharp rise of Jews represents a troubling development, at least insofar as Jews are believed to be living under divine punishment. It is hardly realistic to assert that such a rise is not properly relevant to Christian concerns, or in no way actually threatening to Christians. No doubt, perception and reality were often particularly distant from one another on this issue; untangling the two is one of the more challenging tasks of the historian.

The advent of modern times and their associated liberal, secular values saw a definite shift in attitudes to Jewish influence, since Jews played a large role in modernization. Non-Jews who favored modernization tended to be favorable to Jews, those who feared modernization, unfavorable. At any rate, the following pages will make clear how multiple and often starkly contrasting Jewish actions could feed either the anti- or philo-Semitic vision.

Parallel remarks could be made about Jewish attitudes to non-Jews. Jews who modernized tended to have more favorable attitudes to the non-Jewish world than traditional Jews did. Of course the rise and domination of the Christian nations over the Jewish nation has been a fundamental aspect of Jewish consciousness for nearly two · thousand years; rationalizations for that rise have been gradually incorporated into all varieties of Judaism, even if the modern rise of the Jews along with the establishment of the state of Israel have put the relationship into a different light.

At any rate, the earliest tribalistic and xenophobic elements of Judaism have been modified over the centuries to an important degree by elements of the Jewish tradition that project a more morally complex message of universalistic import, where Jewish difference is viewed as a mystical burden rather than a sign of superior status or special love by God. As the following chapters will show, such differences, perceived and real, have had much to do with the confusions, contradictions, and plain malevolence in the reactions of non-Jews to the presence and persistence of the Jews.

1 ANCIENT AND MEDIEVAL JEW-HATRED

JEW AND NON-JEW: BIBLICAL AND ANCIENT IMAGES OF ENEMIES AND VICTIMS

The earliest, defining contacts of Jew and non-Jew are lost in the mists of the past. What we know with reasonable certainty, according to modern historical standards, about those contacts is finally very little. We do of course have an elaborate and vivid biblical record. However we evaluate the historical reliability of the texts of the Bible, they have had an undeniably profound influence on the way that Jew and non-Jew have perceived and defined one another throughout history.

One early text is of central importance in that regard: the story of Esau (symbolically the non-Jew) and Jacob (symbolically the Jew), twin brothers born to Rebecca and Isaac, as related in the Book of Genesis [*Doc. 1*]. In that account the twins are described as already warring in the womb; later Jacob tricked Esau out of receiving the blessing of their aged and blind father. Esau was the first-born and Isaac's favorite, and when Esau discovered what Jacob had done, he was outraged. Jacob, in fear of his life, fled to distant lands. A lasting hatred was sealed, with symbolic implications for the descendents of Esau and Jacob.

This biblical tale has been the subject of endlessly imaginative commentaries, ones that have discovered messages in the bare text that the uninitiated reader would miss (the 'splendid incoherence' of much of the Old Testament and the need for illuminating commentary on it have been noted by many modern observers [*50 p. 90*]). In rabbinical commentary, Esau has been symbolically and even genetically linked to the adversaries and oppressors of Israel (a name later assumed by Jacob), from the Edomites, Esau's direct descendents, through the Romans, to the nations of modern Europe. That commentary has had to deal with what appears to be a moral paradox, since Jacob seems so obviously at fault for the conflict with his brother, yet Jews recognize Jacob as their spiritual and physical fore-father, as well as the brother favored by God, in the patriarchal line of Abraham, Isaac, Jacob. Esau is portrayed as hairy, crude, and credulous; he is the warrior and hunter, the brutal and uncivilized 'natural man.' Jacob is seen as smooth-skinned, contemplative, and cunning, a man who, in spite of deceiving his father and brother, is somehow seen to represent morality and fidelity to his god's will. Even the trickery is explained away in rabbinical commentary as reflecting that will in subtle ways.

Various long-range conclusions of direct relevance to the history of anti-Semitism have been drawn in Jewish commentary from this earliest confrontation of Jew and non-Jew: 'Esau always hates Jacob' and 'the Messiah will not come until Esau's tears have been exhausted.' In other words, a fundamental line was drawn from the beginning, and with a divine if mystical intent, between Jew and non-Jew. The realm of human harmony and justice will not come until Esau's tears of anger and resentment have been dried – though precisely how that will be accomplished is by no means clear.

This portrayal of Jacob's action as responsible for the hatred he faced from his brother is disconcertingly different from the modern secular portrayal of Jews as innocent victims whose actions or nature have nothing to do with the hatred and misfortunes they have experienced. In fact, most other texts of the Old Testament do not present the Jews as innocent victims. Quite the contrary, those texts typically present Jewish sufferings as punishment for Jewish failings, in particular the repeated laxity of the Jewish people in honoring their god's commandments. That the Gentiles or Other Nations attack the Jews is usually presented as divine punishment for sins arising from within the Jewish nation – again, Jews 'out of control.'

The Other Nations, then, are not usually portrayed as free and responsible agents; they are rather vehicles for an all-powerful god's punishing wrath. This righteous anger flares up in seemingly endless sequences, resulting in punishments of great variety, but most notably in the Jews being conquered and exiled, living then in *galut* (Hebrew for Exile or Diaspora). Time and again – and long after the biblical period – Jewish commentators have stressed that their god is just and thus their sufferings and punishments deserved. If the reasons for the punishment are unclear, or if the punishment scarcely seems to fit the crime – as is certainly often the case – then a mystical purpose is assumed. After the massacres of the Jewish communities of Europe at the beginning of the First Crusade (in 1096), a Jewish chronicler, even while thirsting for vengeance with one voice, recognizes at the same time, that 'the fault is ours! ... Our sins permitted the enemy to triumph; the hand of the Lord weighed heavily upon his people' [137, vol. 1 *p. 85*].

Commentators over the centuries have given the sufferings of Israel many further mystical or seemingly paradoxical dimensions. One has been that the centuries of powerlessness, the terrible tragedies and suffering of the Jews, have been the ultimate foundation for Jewish ethics and the Jewish sense of transcendent purpose as a separate people. As Nobel Prize winner Isaac Bashevis Singer put the matter, 'It ... became clear to me that only in exile did the Jews grow up spiritually' [164 *p. 56*]. Power corrupts, and when tasting power Jews become like the ungodly Other Nations.

In a kindred manner, some Jewish religious thinkers have described anti-Semitism as their god's mystical device to purify and uplift his chosen people. Just as the Jewish god has manipulated the Other Nations to punish his people, so Gentile hatred of Jews is to be understood most fundamentally as a divinely inspired device to prevent Jews from disappearing, from becoming ordinary and blending into the Other Nations. The separatism of the Jews and their inability to forget their origins generate Gentile hostility, while that very hostility contributes to a lasting sense among Jews of unalterable separateness and difference from non-Jews. In short, eternal Jewishness and eternal anti-Semitism are somehow in the nature of things, part of a divine plan. Human efforts to mitigate the mutual hostility, seemingly effective in the short run, are in the long run futile.

In the generations following Jacob and Esau, the Jews are described in the Book of Exodus as becoming slaves of the Egyptian Pharaoh, but again the theme of Jews as hated by others and as victims emerges in ways that are puzzling to modern consciousness. Whether Pharaoh harbors any special hatred for his Israelite slaves is unclear; his refusal to let them go is due to the fact that God 'hardens' the Egyptian ruler's heart. In this regard, Pharaoh appears in a different light than do modern enemies of the Jews. (Most modern commentators, at least, have not described the horrors of Nazi Germany as the result of God's hardening of Hitler's heart, although there are ultra-Orthodox sects that interpret the Holocaust as divine punishment for the Jewish sin of abandoning a strict adherence to traditional religious practices and beliefs.) The main concern of the authors of the Exodus story is ostensibly to demonstrate the power of the Jewish god – more powerful even than the mighty Pharaoh, believed to be a god in human form – rather than to portray the Israelites as innocent victims or morally upright.

Demonstrating that power involved some further moral paradoxes or mysteries: the god of the Jews is described as bringing plagues, natural calamities, and finally the death of the first-born of the people of Egypt, not ostensibly to punish them for their own failings but rather to demonstrate his power and to pressure Pharaoh to free the enslaved Israelites. (That God hardened Pharaoh's heart against freeing them does make for some peculiar logic.) Beyond that, the liberated Israelites themselves are hardly presented as moral paragons; once delivered from slavery, they repeatedly enrage their god as well as their leader Moses by a range of transgressions, among them worshiping the Golden Calf. At one point Moses had to enlist the Levites, the priestly element of the Israelites, to whip them back into line, slaughtering some 3,000 [29 *p. 43*].

Modern Jewish identity is deeply intertwined with the themes of this tale, in particular that 'we were once slaves;' Jews see themselves as identifying with the oppressed and down-trodden, even while at the same time they exult in being God's chosen. In more general ways, Jews come to see themselves as representing a morality of mercy and justice based on their one true god's eternal and immutable laws. But alongside those themes, in Exodus and elsewhere, are ones that tug in opposing directions, that are strongly nationalistic or tribalistic – 'our god is the most powerful!' and 'we Jews have been chosen for a great destiny!'

In the following books of the Bible, those themes are expressed in brutal, genocidal form. The Israelites take over the Promised Land from the native Canaanites. Joshua and his men at Jericho 'utterly destroyed all in the city, both men and women, young and old, oxen, sheep, and asses, with the edge of the sword' (Joshua, 6: 21). The commandment is repeated elsewhere in the Bible that the idol-worshiping peoples of this land were to be annihilated, so that no trace remained of them, their gods, or their revolting practices.

The liberated slaves from Egypt, in short, from being victims become conquerors, imbued with a belief in their religious superiority, carrying out a merciless genocide in the name of their god against the Canaanite idolaters. These apparently contradictory themes would be the object of an ineffably complicated series of justifying interpretations, by Jews and then by Christians, again having to do with divine purposes, often mystically inaccessible to mere mortal reason. But the Jewish god's hand is unmistakably there, guiding the grisly outcome: 'For it was the Lord's doing to harden their [the Canaanites'] hearts that they should come out against Israel in battle, in order that they should be utterly destroyed, and should receive no mercy but be exterminated ...' (Joshua, 11:20).

Later anti-Semites, especially those who rejected Christianity, would find in these tribalistic and murderous narratives much grist for their mills. On the other hand, there are many texts in the later books of the Old Testament that make contrary, universalistic points. The prophet Amos proclaimed that 'God loves you [Israelites] no more than the Philistines [enemies of the Israelites]' (Deut., 8:8). And the direction of later talmudic commentary was that the bloodshed of the conquest of Canaan was a one-time affair never to be repeated on other peoples [71 *pp. 18–19*].

It should also be pointed out that modern historians do not believe that the occupation of Canaan was as dramatic or bloody as the biblical narrative suggests; it was more of a gradual infiltration. There is much evidence in the Bible itself that the extermination was incomplete, since the Israelites are constantly reproached in it for mixing with the Canaanites and – far worse – themselves worshiping Canaanite idols. Similarly, historians point out that the catastrophic events described in Exodus find little or no confirmation in other sources.

There is one non-biblical account of the Exodus story, however, that is particularly interesting in terms of the history of anti-Semitism. It was presented by Manetho, an Egyptian high priest, in the third century BC (a thousand years after the god of the Israelites allegedly so humbled the Pharaoh). He was clearly drawing from earlier Egyptian accounts about the Jews. His version, as well as others that developed parallel to his, was used widely in the ancient world. This Egyptian account offers a strikingly different version of events. It also provides a thought-provoking early glimpse of the mental world of the enemies of Jews. Indeed, Manetho's account of Exodus can be considered a 'classic' text of Jew-hatred: it is one of the earliest; it sets down a number of themes to be picked up by later generations; and it connects with the definition of anti-Semitism provided above, in that it touches upon normal or real tensions between Jews and non-Jews, as well as ones that involve emotionally-driven fantasy about Jews.

Most ancient sources agree that hatred of Jews in the Hellenistic period, when Manetho wrote, was particularly potent in Egypt, especially in Alexandria, his reference point. A major center of trade and learning in the Mediterranean world, Alexandria was culturally and politically dominated by the Greeks, but by the third century it had a mixed population, including Greeks, Jews, Syrians, and native Egyptians. Jews constituted as much as 40 percent of the population, including disproportionate numbers of the wealthy and educated – again, a 'classic' situation, in that Jews throughout history, notably in modern Europe and America, have often been found in large numbers in major cities, and among the wealthier citizens, vulnerable to envy and hatred for their wealth and social position, quite aside from their separatist religious practices [142; 154].

Hostility between Jews and Egyptians flared into bloody clashes, including episodes of extensive rioting. That the Egyptians tended to be on the lower end of the social and economic scale, while the Jews were on the higher end, was plausibly part of the explanation for the intensity of Egyptian–Jewish enmity, though clashes between ruling Greeks and Jews were also common. There were other sources of hostility, ones that might be termed 'religious,' although in the ancient world the modern distinctions between religion, nationality, and culture were not recognized; they were considered to be a whole. In Genesis 8.23, the god of the Jews is recorded as saying that he would 'put a division between my people and your [Egyptian] people.' In other words, these human divisions are again presented as reflecting God's will and plan. The Jews are similarly recorded as observing that 'we … sacrifice to the Lord our God offerings abominable to the Egyptians' (Gen., 8:25). Egyptian religious practices were no less loathsome to the Jews, and in their annual Passover ceremonies, the Jews celebrated the power of their god and the disasters visited upon the Egyptians by that god. More generally, by the third century BC, Judaic prohibition of intimate contact with non-Jews was especially stringent in regard to the Egyptians and the Canaanites.

The Egyptians were a proud and ancient people, and it is hardly surprising that Manetho presented a counter-history of the Egyptian captivity in which the Israelites and their god came out less gloriously than in Exodus. Manetho declared that the Israelites had been driven out of Egypt because they, one of many destitute immigrants who were continually crossing into the Egyptian Empire in times of drought and famine, were afflicted with contagious diseases. The Jews had, over the years, mixed with the native slave population, but were finally ordered out of Egypt by the Pharaoh as a measure of public health. The exclusivity of the Jewish people, Manetho claimed, derived ultimately from their origins as diseased pariahs.

Manetho's tale has the advantage over the biblical account of consistency, plausibility – Egypt had a constant problem with what today would be called illegal aliens – and lack of miracles. But the psychological appeal to Egyptians is the relevant point here: this proud but now somewhat diminished people encountered in their midst a numerous and wealthy 'foreign' population that categorized

Egyptians as especially distasteful 'others' (*goyim*). Imagine, then, the emotional attractions of a story about those pretentious Jews that put them in their place, that exposed their debased and unclean origins.

Competing narratives of this sort were not uncommon in the ancient world, but there was at this time a wide spectrum of reactions by non-Jews, both positive and negative, to the presence of Jews. Similarly, Jews themselves reacted in a range of ways to the non-Jews among whom they lived. One can certainly find in the writings of Jewish religious leaders in this period ample expressions of revulsion and even murderous contempt for the 'idolatrous' peoples among whom they lived, but Jews at this time also mixed with the Other Nations and to varying degrees took up their languages, customs, and religious ideas.

Such was particularly true of the admiring reaction of many Jews to Hellenism, or the civilization of the Greeks, which spread throughout the Mediterranean, after the conquests made by Alexander the Great in the fourth century BC. A revealing example of the powerful attractions of what has been called Greek Wisdom can be found in the historical events that form the background to the modern Jewish celebration of Hanukkah. It commemorates the successful Jewish resistance to what has been described as the forced Hellenization of the Jews by the Greek ruler, Antiochus Epiphanes, in Syria, an area that at the time (second century BC) included Jerusalem. (Hanukkah and Christmas constitute contrasting statements of identity in ways not often realized today, Christmas representing a universalist message, God's love through Christ for all humanity, Hanukkah a particularist one, stressing Jewish chosenness and resistance to 'disappearing' under Hellenistic universalism.)

However, the issue was not only that a Greek ruler tried to force Jews to modify their customs and religion; in truth large numbers of Jews, particularly among the upper classes, had already embraced Hellenistic culture, in particular Greek language and philosophy. Many hoped that Hellenistic and Judaic beliefs could be reconciled. It is moreover clear that Jews have often voluntarily and even enthusiastically embraced the culture of those among whom they have lived; modern America and Europe are only the latest of countless examples. And repeatedly an element of the Jewish population has denounced those tendencies, although in fact these 'fundamentalists' have typically absorbed significant elements of non-Jewish culture themselves, without realizing how much. So in the days of Antiochus Epiphanes, such an element, known to history as the Maccabees, rose up violently. The point often missed is that the Maccabees were battling other Jews – 'collaborators' – at least as much as the Greek leadership.

As the revolt spread, Antiochus's often inept efforts to repress it and pursue his policy of Hellenization also intensified, provoking a popular uprising by the Jews against Greek rule. The result was the restoration of an independent Jewish kingdom and, according to some historians, a decisive preservation of Jewish identity when separatist cultures throughout the eastern Mediterranean were being effectively absorbed into Hellenistic universalism. The Maccabees, or Hasmoneans as the dynasty became known, ruled a revived kingdom of Israel for about a century, until the Romans conquered the area. By that time the Hasmonean kings had provoked much internal dissent and revealed themselves to be as inept as the Greek ruler they had deposed, as well as themselves having embraced the ways of the Greeks to a significant degree.

Jewish resistance to Greek ways had a flip side: many non-Jews in the eastern Mediterranean were attracted to Jewish culture and religion, even while others continued to denounce the Jews as xenophobic, 'enemies of the human race.' By the first century before Christ's birth, Jews were admired in many quarters as a morally disciplined and 'philosophic' people; Jewish practices, such as the Sabbath, and Jewish beliefs, above all ethical monotheism, meshed with similar beliefs and spread far beyond the boundaries of ancient Israel, notably among those admirers or sympathizers (called 'god-fearers') who hesitated to convert to Judaism and join the Jewish people in a total sense by taking up the heavy burden of Jewish rituals (including circumcision). The active recruitment of converts by Jews was more common at this time than it would be for most of the following two thousand years.

These developments help explain how Christianity eventually emerged out of Judaism, but before examining Christianity's origins and the evolution of Christian Jew-hatred, one further biblical text merits attention, the Book of Esther. It offers yet further insights into the origins and evolution of the notion of the 'enemy of Israel' (*sinat yisrael*, the closest Hebrew equivalent of 'anti-Semite'). The Book of Esther seems to have been composed at roughly the same time as the revolt against Antiochus Epiphanes and was almost certainly influenced by it. However, the Book of Esther is set in the Persian court and in an earlier period of Persian rule. An important part of the reason that this story is so important to the history of anti-Semitism is that Haman appears in it: he becomes the symbolic arch-enemy of the Jews for the centuries to follow.

The authors of the Book of Esther present Haman, the vizier or highest minister of the Persian king, Ahasuerus (Xerxes in Greek), in a different light than Pharaoh or Antiochus. He is not described as a tool of the Jewish god, nor does that god intervene or express his will. Indeed, the Book of Esther is unusual among the books of the Bible for its lack of any mention of God or Jewish religious values; it provides instead a purely secular tale, describing the Jewish people in danger of mass destruction but then saved dramatically, entirely by human agency. This story is now recounted annually in the Feast of Purim, during which any mention of Haman's name is greeted by foot-stamping and noise-making.

The authors of the Book of Esther confused a number of historical details, while transparently making up others. Historical accuracy was not their concern; they composed something like a modern historical novel, and the deeper significance of the narrative, a source of its lasting attraction to Jews over the years, has not been historical but psychological, speaking to powerful emotional needs: time and again Jews would face terrible enemies and threats of destruction, meeting defeat, humiliation, and dispersal. In the Book of Esther the Jews win.

Revealingly, Haman is described as a descendent of the Amalekites, a tribe described as having treacherously attacked the Israelites as they wandered in the wilderness of Sinai; thereafter they remained traditional enemies of Jewish kings. Amalek, like his descendent, Haman, becomes in later rabbinical commentary a symbol of the most unqualified kind of evil, the most dangerous and reviled enemy of the Jews. Yet the extent to which Haman's hatred of the Jews in Persia was hereditary or tribalistic is difficult to determine from the text, since in it the most clearly presented reason that Haman turned on the Jews was that their leader, Mordecai, offended him publicly: 'And when Haman saw that Mordecai did not bow down or do obeisance to him, Haman was filled with fury.' In fact, these wooden and laconic lines seem to suggest that Haman had been unaware of the existence of the Jews up to that point: his advisers 'made known to him the people of Mordecai, [and] Haman sought to destroy all the Jews, the people of Mordecai.' Haman then reported to his king, in a celebrated or 'classic' passage, echoing down the centuries:

There is a certain people. ... Their laws are different from those of every other people, and they do not keep the king's laws, so that it is not to the king's profit to tolerate them. (Esther, 3: 6–8)

What is striking is that the Jews are not described as refusing to worship another god; they are simply 'different' and 'do not keep the king's laws,' which could mean anything from cultural peculiarities to subversion. Similarly, the rescue of the Jews from Haman's designs is presented in entirely secular ways. It is accomplished through the intrigues of the beautiful Esther (Mordecai's niece), who charms the king and becomes his queen, without revealing her Jewish identity. She then succeeds in turning the king against Haman.

The bare text also leaves unexplained what it is that makes Haman so clearly evil. His anger at what appears to be an almost unbelievable provocation by Mordecai hardly makes it clear that he deserves his subsequent status of arch-fiend. Nor is it made clear why Mordecai and Esther are good, except of course from a tribalistic standpoint, since Haman is a descendent of Amalek, while Mordecai is a descendent of the Jewish King Saul. Throughout the text, little or nothing is said about the beliefs and moral qualities of Mordecai and Esther, or the nature of the Jewish people.

At any rate, once Esther had been able to turn the tables on Haman, the Jews were allowed by the king to carry out a wholesale retribution. Haman and his ten sons were publicly hung, and throughout the kingdom some 75,000 of Haman's supporters were put to death – a spectacular bloodbath, if the figures could be believed, but again what is interesting is the secular nature of the violence. This mass slaughter is not presented as divinely orchestrated by the need to clear the land of loathsome idolaters but rather as one tribe wiping out another that had planned to wipe it out.

From Esau to Pharaoh to Antiochus Epiphanes to Haman, the 'enemies of Israel' appear in a disorienting number of guises, with few common traits: Esau, an ignorant brute, yet also a brother, with an all-too understandable grievance; Pharaoh, an oppressive god-king who is nonetheless a mere puppet of the Jewish god; Antiochus, a Hellenizing despot out to destroy Jewish religion and culture; and Haman, a chief minister driven by a personal affront and tribal memories. What it is precisely that makes each of them wicked remains elusive, as is indeed the conceptualization of evil itself, beyond the tautology that the evil ones are those who have hated Jews.

Similarly, the reasons that these figures have hated the Jews are by no means presented in coherent ways. Esau's anger at being tricked seems understandable enough – hardly the result of some ignorant or baseless fantasy about Jacob – while Pharaoh's oppression of the Israelites seems part of a divine plan of morally tortuous and mystifying dimensions. Manetho actually presents a more cogent and plausible perspective, in which hostility to the Israelite slaves is again perfectly understandable: they were diseased members of the lowest orders of society who subsequently hide that ignoble past, finally becoming separatists and disdainful of others. Haman denounces the Jews as vaguely 'different,' possibly a threat to public order, but his evil designs for them seem most plausibly to derive from the fact that the Jew Mordecai has insulted him and also because of tribalistic animosities. Antiochus Epiphanes sees the Jews as superstitious separatists, causing public unrest and irrationally refusing to embrace the benefits of Hellenistic civilization – again hardly baseless fantasies or incomprehensible motives on his part.

Whatever these seeming contradictions and blurred images, nowadays the most commonly encountered explanation for the hatred the Jews experienced in ancient times, as subsequently, is that they were 'different,' stubbornly attached to their god and his dictates. As one of the first modern historians of anti-Semitism summarized the matter.

> Jews were hated ... because they never entered any city as citizens but always as a privileged class. ... They separated themselves from other inhabitants by their rituals and customs. They considered the soil of other nations impure [and] ... entertained no strangers for fear of pollution. The mystery with which they surrounded themselves excited curiosity as well as aversion. [101 *pp. 20–1*]

Several aspects of this explanation need to be pointed out, since they underline the difference of pre-Christian hostility from the hatred of Jews that developed after the birth of Christ. In the ancient world, the Jews were not seen as innocent or defenseless victims. On the contrary, they were considered to be impossibly contentious and unusually inclined to violence. Suspicion of them by various rulers, then, might be termed 'normal,' hardly mysterious. Similarly, popular dislike of Jews because they kept to themselves, denigrating other peoples and religions, is hardly surprising; suspicion of those who are different is a universal human trait, and those who denigrate others do not usually win affection for that trait.

THE UNIQUENESS OF CHRISTIAN JEW-HATRED

Persecution of Jews existed in the ancient world; they were conquered, oppressed, and scattered, but they were not marked out for persecution in quite the same way as they would be under

Christian rule. Similarly, some of the myths in the ancient world charged the Jews with demonic practices. They were accused, for example, of murdering non-Jews for secret, cannibalistic rituals. And Manetho's tale of their spreading disease has connections with later charges of how they 'infected' the people among whom they lived. But an emotion-charged picture of the Jew as uniquely destructive and aligned in dark, frightening ways with the Evil One gradually evolved in peculiar directions with the advent of Christianity.

Jesus and his disciples were of course Jews, and they were at first denounced and persecuted by Jewish authorities as a dissident, indeed heretical Jewish sect whose members deserved death. But once Christianity began to gain power, inheriting Judaism's sense of intolerant righteousness, it persecuted the Jews in turn. Still, that transformation, the process by which Christianity and Judaism defined one another – changing places as persecutor and persecuted – was involved and enduringly ambiguous. It may be said to be still under-way to this very day.

Initially Christ and his followers were dismissed by Jewish religious leaders as insignificant if also particularly outrageous dissidents. Jesus was a common laborer, almost certainly illiterate, and as such completely unqualified to be a Jewish religious leader. His followers were dismissed as a credulous rabble, believing things that were deeply alien to Jewish tradition, in particular that a man was also a god. According to the Talmud, Jesus was appropriately condemned to death by a rabbinical court for idolatry and for an outrageous contempt for rabbinical authority [159 *pp. 97–8*]. Crucifixion, the method by which Jesus was later known to be executed, was Roman rather than Jewish, and in the New Testament the various accounts describe the death penalty as carried out by the Romans, who ruled Palestine at this time. Nonetheless, according to those accounts, the crucifixion was not only instigated by the Jews but heartily applauded by them.

The apostle Paul, generally considered the founder of Christianity after Christ's death, was himself at first a zealous Jewish persecutor of the Christians, but a blinding vision of Christ led him into the ranks of those he had been oppressing. Paul and the other first Christians claimed to be 'true Jews,' God's new chosen people. He also blended into Christian belief elements that came from the non-Jewish, Hellenistic worldview, in particular the notion of a divine messiah bringing universal salvation. Such a messiah was different in funda-mental ways from the traditional Jewish belief in a messiah as a national leader, a human being who would be carrying out the will of

God. The writers of the Gospels continued the process of transforming Christianity from a highly problematic Jewish sect into a fiercely anti-Jewish religion, in the process attracting an increasingly non-Jewish following.

Christianity remained weak and vulnerable for several centuries after Jesus' death, persecuted on nearly all sides, and often confused with Judaism by the Roman authorities and other observers. However, Christian missionaries made steady inroads, particularly in the ranks of the previously mentioned 'god-fearing' admirers of Jewish beliefs and practices. A decisive step occurred in the fourth century, when the Emperor Constantine himself accepted Christian beliefs, however ambiguously.

In the process of emerging from a persecuted sect to a state-supported religion, Christianity evolved in ways that rendered it scarcely recognizable from its first-century origins. Its major interpreters, the Church Fathers, all devoted much attention to defining how Christianity had superseded Judaism. Their writings entailed an elaborate and often harshly worded denigration of Judaism and of the Jews. Jewish religious leaders were at first relatively unconcerned with this upstart religion, but as Christianity's attacks grew, as did its power, expressions of hatred for it by Jewish writers, too, became more vitriolic, including demands to burn Christian scriptures and a notorious description of Christ as having committed various sexual perversions and as being condemned to boil in excrement in hell [159 p. 21].

In spite of this war of words, physical attacks on the Jews remained exceptional in the first thousand years of Christianity. In those years, Christians grew vastly in numbers and in political power, while Jewish numbers plummeted, in both relative and absolute terms. And Jews faced repeated humiliations. Before the birth of Christ, they had been defeated by the Romans, their country taken over; revolts against the Romans after Christ's birth finally resulted in the Jews being driven from their homeland and their temple demolished. These events were interpreted by Christians as unmistakable signs of God's displeasure with the Jews for having rejected Christ.

The continuing and massive decline in Jewish numbers, reputation, and power over the centuries fundamentally altered the nature of the relationship with Christians, and later with Moslems. Jews came to fit ever more into the category of defenseless victim; they could less and less realistically entertain the notion of fighting back. Accommodations of various sorts, practical and theoretical, with those in power became ever more necessary to Jewish survival. The earlier charge of idolatry against the Christians gradually receded. That the Christians and the Moslems worshiped the same god as the Jews was gradually recognized by Jewish religious leaders.

The survival of Jews, in however dwindling numbers and general esteem, was itself a challenge, indeed a troubling mystery to Christians. It needed to be explained and justified in terms of Christian belief. Some Christians argued that Jews should be put to death if they persisted in their denigration of Christian truth, but for the most part leading Christians urged that Jews not be physically attacked or even forced to convert. And that position gradually became the official policy of the Church, effectively continuing the policies of the Roman Empire which, in spite of several violent episodes, generally protected the Jews and even recognized special privileges in their regard.

The Christian position was worked out in significant part by Saint Augustine, the most important of the Church Fathers, who lived in the fourth century. He added a number of philosophically sophisti-cated embellishments to the charges against the Jews, and he described them as carnal, blind to spirituality, and corrupted by hatred of non-Jews. He agreed that Jews deserved death but argued that they should be allowed by Christians to survive as 'witnesses,' living evidence, in their sufferings and degradation, of the truth and superiority of Christianity. Of course control of them by special laws reflecting their degraded status would be necessary.

The charge of deicide, or 'killing god,' already present in the New Testament, was further developed by Saint Augustine, as indeed by most Church Fathers. Among them, perhaps the most notorious for his attacks on Jews and Judaism was Saint John Chrysostom. Living in Antioch in Asia Minor, another major city of the ancient world, in the fourth century, he was especially noted for his eloquence. His tirades against the Jews, given to large and admiring crowds, are revealing in a number of regards. They illustrate, for example, the extent to which the rivalry between Judaism and Christianity was still alive in the late fourth century. In a famous sermon, John stated the matter with disarming directness: 'If you admire the Jewish way of life, what do you have in common with us? If the Jewish rites are holy and venerable, our way of life must be false' [181 *p. 68*]. He, like Augustine, complained bitterly about what he viewed as the un-believable insolence of Jews: 'The cross is ridiculed ... the son insulted, the grace of the Spirit rejected ...' [182 *p. 97*].

Nonetheless, even John recognized important Jewish virtues, and, interestingly, for all his poisonous invective, he did not urge his listeners to attack Jews physically. There were no riots or other kinds of physical attacks in direct response to John's preaching. But there can be little question that John contributed significantly to an enduringly potent tradition of Christian hatred for Jews and Judaism: the Jews had not only clamored for the murder of Christ; they now continued to rejoice in that bloody death. Jews hated the Son of God as they detested His message of universal salvation, which involved a demotion or dethronement of the Jews as the chosen people. And of course they hated Christians for claiming to be God's new chosen.

Such charges evolved in obscure channels over the centuries to the ever more widely accepted charge by the high middle ages that Jews sought ways to torture and kill individual Christians, as Christ had been tortured and killed centuries before. From such notions even more fantastic beliefs evolved: the Blood Libel (that Jews used the blood of Christians for matzos at Passover) and the Desecration of the Host (that Jews befouled Communion wafers, believed by Christians to be mystically the body of Christ).

From the eleventh century on, the charge that Jews plotted to do physical harm to Christians spread with particular strength in areas of northern France, southern Germany, and England. This charge has been described by some historians as a decisive, portentous step in the evolution of anti-Semitism in Europe, presaging the Holocaust in its physical violence and its peculiar demonization of the Jews [32]. Jewish settlements in those areas of Europe had been sparse in the early medieval period, but by the eleventh century significant numbers of Jews had emigrated from the Mediterranean, ostensibly attracted by economic opportunity. Initially, most came as merchants, but over the years many Jews turned to money-lending, and some of them became wealthy, a few extremely so, usually protected and given privileges by kings and nobles.

Such a rise in fortunes of those supposedly condemned by God to degradation inevitably raised troubling questions for Christians who accepted Augustine's doctrine. It is plausible that the role of money-lender – hated and considered exploitative ('blood-sucking') in nearly all cultures – added substance and force to the evolving suspicions and resentments of Jews as deniers and murderers of Christ. Such notions then blended into the fantastic charges of the ritual murder of His followers, conceived by Christians as mystically one with Him.

The violent attacks on Jews, beginning with the First Crusade (1096), were rationalized with Christian language ('why journey to the Holy Land to defeat the infidel when the murderers of Christ are here in our midst?'), but elements of what would now be termed ethnic hostility almost certainly played a role. The Jews were visibly different, recent arrivals, growing in numbers, and speaking unfamiliar languages. There was as well among Christians a simple desire for plunder, to rob the Jews of their newly acquired wealth. Revealingly, Christian religious and civil authorities condemned these attacks, and in some instances were able to protect the Jews. However, the armed and often lawless Crusaders, joined by turbulent mobs, frequently paid little heed to those authorities, and indeed violently attacked many others than the Jews. Similarly, both religious and secular authorities condemned the Blood Libel, affirming that it had no foundation in Jewish religion, but those condemnations seem to have done little to halt the spread of that fantastic belief among Christians.

Demonization of the Jews developed in the following five hundred years of European history, which were also marked by recurring violent outbreaks against Jewish settlements and expulsions from major areas of western Europe. The middle years of the fourteenth century were marked by major outbreaks of the bubonic plague, wiping out millions, perhaps as much as half of Europe's population, and Jews were often blamed for spreading it by poisoning wells. Again, the denunciation of these charges as false by Christian authorities did not prevent the spread of belief in them.

The religious wars of the seventeenth century were once again hugely destructive, with Jews often caught in the middle of the various warring Christian sects. The association of the Jew with demonic forces, the belief that Jews were not only religious dissenters but physically dangerous to Christians, had spread widely and sunk in deeply.

On the other hand, this bleak picture did not prevail everywhere. Jews survived in many areas of central Europe; not all Christians accepted such sweeping demonization of them. While Jews were being expelled from many areas of western Europe, they were being invited to settle in others, especially in Poland, where the kings and nobles welcomed their skills and economic acumen. Jews in Poland during the late medieval and early modern period experienced what has been described as 'heaven,' a golden age. They prospered economically, grew remarkably in numbers, and developed impressive centers of Jewish learning.

If Christian allies had been entirely lacking, if all Christians had accepted the more extreme forms of demonization, the Jews of Europe simply could not have survived. Many Christians continued to find Jews 'useful;' economically Jews served purposes that were widely valued. Jewish doctors were consulted by many, including kings, nobles, and even prelates. Beyond that, it seems that simple human contact often defied religious prejudice. Jews and non-Jews often mixed in various ways that their religions frowned upon, each finding the other not only materially useful but humanly estimable or at least tolerable.

Even where Jews faced violent attacks, those attacks cannot be described as exclusively the result of Christian fantasies, having absolutely nothing to do with Jewish actions or nature, especially when Jews were wealthy and identified with oppressive rulers. Normal tensions remained, mixed into the fantasies and exaggerated by them. Recognizing the relative powerlessness and vulnerability of Jews should not lead to the conclusion that there was no longer any kind of mutuality between Jew and non-Jew in the tensions that developed between them. An historian has recently observed that 'medieval Jews despised the faith of the Christian majority and expressed their animus in terms as vigorous as those used by Christians in denouncing Judaism' [32 *p. 102*], while another has pointed to a trend among some Jews at this time toward 'vengeful messianism,' looking to violence against their enemies [cited in 32 *p. 75*].

However, the most frequently maintained position by historians of anti-Semitism has remained that normal hatreds and mutually provoked conflict were not the decisive issue in these medieval attacks on Jews. What was crucial, according to those historians, were the myths and fantasies about Jews that were developing within the psyches of European Christians independent of anything the Jews were or did; the above-quoted historian concludes that 'prejudice and persecution are ultimately grounded far more in the circumstances of the persecuting majority than in the behavior of the persecuted minority' [32 *p. 77*].

The point is debatable, but it is nonetheless true that belief systems develop according to a logic all their own – if 'logic' is the proper word – driven by obscure psychological agendas. A related point has been made above, in regard to the appeals of various biblical or anti-biblical texts: what is actually stated in them is less important than what subsequent interpreters make of them. It is true that Christian fantasies expanded or intensified in many regards, that the middle ages in Europe were characterized by a growing intolerance, a narrowing definition of acceptable belief. Such a narrowing was applicable not only to Jews but many other 'outsiders' – heretic Christians more than Jews – but also homosexuals and lepers. But in these years, fantasies about Jews continued to be fed by realities, in a complex and nearly impenetrable interplay.

A related issue is the degree to which Christian persecution was responsible for the hostility to Christianity by Jews. There is little question that Jewish anger and resentment were aggravated by Christian attacks, but, as we have seen, Jewish hatred and derision for Christians both predated and developed to an important degree independently of Christian persecution. The process was not essentially different from the way that Christian hatred for Jews developed according to its own logic and not only in reaction to Jewish provocation. Many of the most hate-filled Jewish texts date from the time when Christianity was still weak and hardly capable of mounting significant physical attacks on the Jews.

When, by the high middle ages, Christians began to appreciate the extent to which, in the words of one historian, 'that Jews had been mocking them for centuries' in the Talmud and other rabbinical works, they were outraged [77 *p. 34*]. Copies of the Talmud were burned on a number of occasions, just as copies of the Gospels had been earlier destroyed by Jewish authorities when they had the power to do so.

THE END OF THE MEDIEVAL WORLD

The Protestant Reformation marked the beginning of ever more pluralistic Christian attitudes to Jews. In some regards the break-up of the Catholic Church was good news for the Jews, especially insofar as the Protestant sects returned to Old Testament models; Protestants who thought of themselves as 'Israelites' often tended toward a form of philo-Semitism, although the fundamentally anti-Judaic elements of Christian doctrine could not be easily ignored. And Martin Luther [*Doc. 3*], who, as it were, started it all, was anything but a friend to Jews. When his initially cordial overtures to them, envisaging their conversion to his understanding of Christianity, were rebuffed, he responded with murderous fury, in words that uncannily seem to presage Nazi atrocities. Yet even in this instance of seemingly genocidal hatred, it is unclear that Lutheran Christianity as such significantly engendered anti-Jewish attitudes. Some of the least anti-Semitic nations in Europe, including Denmark, Norway, and Sweden, were predominantly Lutheran. Luther's diatribes against the Jews were not accepted by other Lutherans in Germany, even in his own day, and not taught to Lutheran congregations. To be sure, from the late nineteenth century on, anti-Semites used Luther's writings to support their positions, but that retrospective use, which undoubtedly helped to legitimate anti-Semitic positions, is different from a deeper and longer tradition that made anti-Semitism inevitable among Lutherans.

In the religious wars that grew out of the Reformation, Europe came close to committing suicide; murderous intolerance raged not only between Catholic and Protestant but within Protestant denominations, until much of Europe was reduced to smoking ruins and untold millions had perished. Jews were often caught in the crossfire of the various warring factions. The greatest massacre of Jews in Europe before the Holocaust occurred when the Ukrainian leader, Bogdan Chmielnicki, in a rebellion against Polish overlords, Catholic clergy, and the Jews who typically acted as agents of the Polish upper classes, exacted a wanton and bloody retribution. However, the older accounts of the Chmielnicki massacres, which spoke of hundreds of thousands of Jewish dead [*Doc. 4*], have been put into serious question by modern scholarship. One recent painstaking account has concluded that most Jews were able to avoid violence; this period was 'a brutal but relatively short interruption in the steady growth and expansion of Polish Jewry' [81 *p. 121*] Indeed, the large numbers of Jews in Poland by the eighteenth century could not have been attained had Jews died in the seventeenth century in anything like the numbers once claimed.

The other major tragedy at the end of the middle ages was the mass expulsion of Jews from Spain in 1492. Even more than in Poland, Jews had prospered in Spain and came to constitute a large part of the population, entering into high political office and blending into the general population through both voluntary and forced conversions. Following the expulsion orders, most emigrated to various Mediterranean destinations ruled by Islam, but a few made their way to Europe and even the Americas. Their branch of Jewry, termed Sephardic, thereafter became a small but illustrious branch of European Jewry. Just as Polish Jews absorbed a number of cultural traits from Poland, so Sephardic Jews were known for their 'Spanish' traits, among them pride of lineage. One historian notes that the Sephardic Jews' preoccupations with 'purity of blood' meant that they refused, well into the eighteenth century, to intermarry with non-Sephardic Jews, or indeed even to handle dishes that Ashkenazic (German and Polish) Jews, with their 'impure blood' had touched [134 *p. 380–2*]. There was no little irony in such attitudes, since Jews who had converted to Christianity in Spain themselves often faced the charge that their 'impure' Jewish blood made them uncertain or questionable Christians.

2 THE COMING OF MODERN TIMES

THE ENLIGHTENMENT AND THE GROWTH OF TOLERANCE

The memory of the medieval and early modern periods was not a happy one for the *philosophes*, the tone-setting intellectuals of the late seventeenth and eighteenth centuries, a period that has been called the Enlightenment. The term was chosen to emphasize its difference from the medieval 'dark ages.' Dennis Diderot, a prominent *philosophe* of the mid-eighteenth century, spoke for many others when he wrote that 'never has any religion been so fecund in crime as Christianity. ... The abominable cross has caused blood to flow on every side.' One might assume that such a judgement would be 'good for the Jews,' and in some regards it was. But there was much more to the story; Enlightened ideals, like those of Protestantism, represented a paradoxical mix of good and bad prospects for the Jews.

By the closing decades of the seventeenth century, there emerged a growing belief in the need for religious toleration if European civilization was to survive. This belief reflected a break from previously dominant themes of the Judeo-Christian tradition, with its monotheistic claim to exclusive possession of truth and righteousness; it also reflected a renewed respect for the Hellenistic and Roman world, with its willingness to recognize and tolerate many ways to truth and many visions of God.

The earlier dethronement of the Jews by the Christians was now taken a step further: the Christians had declared that the Jews were no longer God's Chosen People; the *philosophes* argued that the Jews never had been a chosen people – indeed that the concept was absurd. For Enlightened thinkers the crude and contradictory images of the deity in the Old Testament reflected the mental processes of a primitive people who conceived of God as a 'cruel and capricious tyrant,' in the words of Edward Gibbon, the celebrated eighteenth-century historian of the fall of Rome and rise of Christianity.

An important contributor to this process of dethronement was himself a Jew, Baruch Spinoza. His writings suggest how much the ideals of the Enlightenment, the belief in the powers of human reason in contrast to the revealed truths of religion, had begun already by the middle years of the previous century to penetrate the ranks of both Jew and non-Jew. He contributed significantly to the discussion in leading intellectual circles about the historical reliability and logical coher-ence of the Old Testament. Not surprisingly, he was excommunicated in 1656 from the Jewish community to which he belonged in Amsterdam, for his 'wrong opinions' and 'horrible heresies,' with the following words:

> By the anathema with which Joshua banned Jericho [leading to the slaughter of all its inhabitants]. ... The anger and wrath of the Lord will rage against this man, and bring all the curses that are written in the Book of the Law. ... We order that nobody should communicate with him ... or stay under the same roof ... or read anything composed or written by him. [122 *p. 57*]

Spinoza was not harmed physically; the implicit call for his death in this decree did not correspond to the practices of Jewish communities in most of western Europe, although floggings and other forms of violent punishment of Jewish non-conformists were still practiced in Jewish communities well into the eighteenth century in eastern Europe.

The tolerant trends of the Enlightenment were not accompanied by sympathy on the part of the *philosophes* for Jews as Jews, as distinguished from Jews as victims of intolerance and persecution. And most evidence suggests that an 'unenlightened' suspicion of Jews among the ordinary mass of the Christian population remained through the next century and well into the twentieth; those who embraced the principles of reason and toleration were a numerically insignificant minority of intellectuals, although one of growing influence in the long run.

The 'Jewish question', as it eventually became known, was widely discussed in the intellectual and governing circles of Europe toward the end of the eighteenth century. While a number of non-Jews spoke up for a fairer treatment of Europe's Jews, few had favorable comments about contemporary Judaism or about Jews in their present state. Even those who believed that legal discrimination against Jews should be abolished nonetheless considered most Jews to be of low moral character – cunning and dishonest – while Judaism was hidebound and itself bigoted. Indeed, even those Jews who spoke up to defend their people often did so in remarkably back-handed ways. They granted the Jewish population suffered from all too obvious defects, both moral and physical, but insisted that those defects were due to centuries of persecution and would disappear once that persecution came to an end.

This enduring suspicion of Jews on the part of an elite of highly educated people who prided themselves in being tolerant and enlightened suggests some provocative questions. If their animosity was not driven by Christian myths, and if they did not demonize Jews as Christians had, can we continue to term this hostility 'unique' in the sense so far suggested? Indeed, can their attitudes still be described as deriving primarily from 'fantasy' rather than 'reality'? The example of Voltaire, a man who has often been considered the symbol of the Enlightenment, suggests just how elusive answers to these questions can be.

Voltaire devoted much of his life to denouncing bigotry, particularly that of the Catholic Church. He also attacked the Jews and Judaism as no less bigoted. There was of course a major difference: the Church banned his books and threatened him in other regards; the rabbis were in no position to do anything of the sort to him. Banning Voltaire's books was not much of an issue for them, at any rate, because traditional Jewish authorities had long warned against reading any books by non-Jewish authors.

Voltaire was witty and entertaining; he wrote rapidly and prolifically, but consistency, profundity, or careful study of the subjects at hand were not his strong points. Isolated quotations from his many works can suggest contradictory conclusions about his beliefs. A key point about those beliefs, as about those of most *philosophes*, is that he saw no divine purpose to Jewish existence, whereas Christian thinkers believed that God had initially chosen the Jews as His people and that Jewish survival in Christendom was part of a divine plan. Voltaire did not consider the survival of the Jews to be desirable; he looked to a time when the Jews, like the Christians, would finally disappear by voluntarily merging into a society of common humanity and reason.

Voltaire did not believe that force was justified to assure the victory of his cause. In one of the most quoted passages of his *Philosophical Dictionary*, he describes the Jews as 'an ignorant and barbarous people, who have long united the most sordid avarice with the most detestable superstition and the most invincible hatred for every people by whom they are tolerated and enriched.' But he added, 'we ought not to burn them' [106 *p. 41*].

Voltaire's judgements were often based on ignorance, but his 'fantasies' about Jews were not of the same quality as Christian fantasies; he did not demonize Jews with a mystically potent imagery. They were for him human beings, historically stubborn perpetuators of dangerous and socially disruptive principles, to be sure, but not servants of the Evil One. In this regard, his attitude was a return to those of the ancient world, when Jews were generally considered human antagonists not demons; hostility to them usually had a plausible relationship to their actual nature. Similarly, Voltaire himself claimed to see Jews according to evidence of the senses, keeping an open mind, not according to texts that were considered sacred and infallible. In a revealing exchange with the noted Jewish philosopher and economist Isaac de Pinto, Voltaire apologized in terms that are hard to imagine coming from the pen of religious leaders of the past, Christian or Jewish:

> When a man is in the wrong, he should make reparations for it, and I was in the wrong in attributing to a whole nation the vices of some individuals. ... Superstition has caused so many Jews and Christians to be slaughtered. ... As you are a Jew, remain so. But be a philosopher. This is my best wish to you in this short life. [122 *p. 308*]

These words further underline how problematic it is to include Voltaire in the ranks of the Hamans, the great Jew-haters of history. His hostility was based on a belief that the Jews themselves had historically represented intolerance, a rejection of human solidarity, and a denial of the reliability of human reason to rise above revealed truths. While it is true that he was ignorant of the variety and subtlety of Jewish thought, it seems unjustified to describe his beliefs about Jews as blind prejudice, or dogmatic and ignorant fantasies having absolutely no relationship with what Jews were actually like in his own lifetime or in the past.

There were a few *philosophes* who could be described as philo-Semitic. This kind of Enlightened benevolence toward Jews went distinctly beyond the Christian recognition of Jewish value as testimony to Christian truth or the more practical sense that some Jews could be useful economically. The most famous exponent of this variety of philo-Semitism was Gotthold Lessing, a major figure of the German Enlightenment, whose plays, *The Jews* (1754) and *Nathan the Wise* (1779), had as protagonists admirable or heroic Jews. This was a distinct departure from European literature up to that point, in which Jewish villains were the rule. Lessing's wise Jew, Nathan, indeed, was presented as someone who defended Enlightened tolerance and rationality against Christian bigotry.

However, this image was scarcely less remote from what most Jews were actually like and no more based on a deep and detailed knowledge of Judaism than those offered by Voltaire. The character Nathan was widely understood to be based on a living Jew, Moses Mendelssohn, who was indeed an Enlightened man, widely admired and befriended by a number of leading intellectuals of the day. But he was also understood to be highly exceptional, proof of the possibility of Jewish Enlightenment and reform, not an example of what most Jews were actually like. In fact, Mendelssohn himself continued to live as a traditional Jew, although his famous translation of the Old Testament into German (using Hebrew characters) was remarkable for the extent to which it ignored traditional Jewish commentary. And if praised by some Gentiles, Mendelssohn was vehemently condemned by most traditional Jewish leaders.

THE FRENCH REVOLUTION AND THE JEWS

These idealized and rather inconclusive discussions about the Jews by men like Voltaire and Lessing took on more pressing dimensions in 1789, when revolutionaries took over in France. In the name of the ideals of the Enlightenment, they declared feudalism at an end. Eventually they overturned kings, nobles, and churchmen; they wrote constitutions, redrew national boundaries, and even altered the calendar. In this dazzling flurry of revolutionary activity, it was inevitable that they would also address the issue of the special laws governing the Jews. Such an agenda was implicit in the abolition of feudalism, since Jews in France and elsewhere had been legally defined in a feudal manner, that is, as a separate entity, the Jewish nation with its own laws and privileges, owing fealty to the king, not to the Christian nations within which they lived.

However, the notion of Jews as equal citizens under the law caused a number of delegates to the revolutionary National Assembly to balk. The hesitation existed on both the left and on the right. Indeed, Jewish religious leaders in France themselves also expressed large reservations, fearing that civil equality for Jews would work to dissolve the old bonds of Jews to one another and establish new, stronger ones to the French state and people. Many observers concluded that it would be wiser simply to recognize them as resident aliens, removing the often humiliating restrictions on Jewish economic activity. Full citizenship for Jews was too radical a step.

Both Jews and non-Jews emphasized that Jews everywhere constituted a separate nation, 'a people apart' under traditional Jewish law, never to be blended with others, at least not until the messiah came. Many aspects of that traditional law gave pause to the delegates. They remarked, for example, that Jews would be incapable of fulfilling their duties as citizens because they could not by their laws serve in the French army. Their dietary laws forbade them to eat the food that other Frenchmen ate, and they could not drink any wine produced by Gentiles. They were forbidden to work or fight on their Sabbath. Such laws were indeed clearly intended to preserve Jewish separation from non-Jews.

A left-wing delegate from the northeastern province of Alsace, a largely German-speaking area in which the great majority of Jews in France lived, expressed complete agreement with the general revolutionary principle that all inhabitants of France, whether Catholic or Protestant, French-speaking or not, should be granted citizenship. But he objected that Jews were different: Judaism was not a universalistic religion in the way that Christian denominations were; it was an all-embracing way of life for a people who had been self-consciously separatist for thousands of years. Most Jews did not think of themselves as members of the French people or nation. Indeed, most Jews in Alsace felt far closer to Jews living across the border in Germany than they did to Christians in France. He insisted that 'it is not I that exclude the Jews; they exclude themselves' [69 *p. 16*].

Many delegates agreed, but there was also a recognition that at least some Jews no longer fitted into that self-excluding category, since Judaism, no less than Christianity, was in transformation and turmoil. Major differences existed among the Ashkenazim and Sephardim. The latter lived mostly in scattered settlements in the south of France; their numbers were smaller and they had already substantially assimilated into French language and culture by the time of the Revolution. The Ashkenazim, who constituted over 80 percent of the Jews in France, lived mostly in Alsace. The language that most of them spoke, Yiddish, was closely related to German. They tended to be poorer than the Sephardim, more observant of religious tradition, and in other regards, such as dress, were visibly not part of the surrounding people. The Sephardim had moved into a wider variety of professions and economic activities, whereas the Ashkenazim remained largely connected with their traditional economic roles, including that of money-lender.

It emerged from the debates in the National Assembly that there was relatively little opposition to giving civil equality to the Sephardim, but the Ashkenazim were a different matter. The delegates from Alsace, arguing that they had first-hand knowledge of the Jews in question, persisted in their objections. That the Sephardim were given civil equality first and without much controversy points to an interesting detail: it did not appear to be Jewishness as such that bothered most delegates; it was rather the specific kind of Jews in question, as well as their numbers and concentration. That a number of Sephardim seconded the descriptions of the Ashkenazim as hide-bound and superstitious further strengthened the point that the Ashkenazim were unacceptable as citizens.

Ultimately, civil equality to all French residents was incorporated into the new constitution adopted in 1791; a majority of the delegates voted in favor of giving the Ashkenazim equal rights, more out of a desire to be consistent with universalistic revolutionary principles than a sincere belief that Ashkenazic Jews were presently suited to become genuine French citizens. The heady optimism of those first revolutionary years inclined many delegates to believe anything was possible, even reforming the Jews.

Nonetheless, the issue of the Alsatian Jews remained a sore point. More than a decade later, after Napoleon had assumed leadership of the country, bitter complaints were presented to him that the Jews of Alsace had in truth not used their new-found equality to reform themselves. Quite the opposite, they used that equality to expand their old practices of deception and exploitation of the common people. Napoleon by this time was considered by Jews in many parts of Europe as their liberator, since occupation by his armies generally meant the breaking down of ghetto walls and the introduction of French law. But in fact Napoleon sympathized with the complaints that reached him. He expressed impatience with the idealized assumptions made about the humanity of the Jews by their defenders in the first years of the revolution. He now insisted on 'facts'. What were Jews' actual beliefs and actions? In 1806, he summoned the Assembly of Jewish Notables and presented to them a series of pointed questions, ones that returned to many of the issues so hotly contested in the discussions before 1791.

Napoleon brought up again, for example, the issue of whether Jews were capable of sincerely embracing French nationality over Jewish national traditions. Did they in truth consider Christians in France closer to them than the Jews of other nations? He asked whether Jews followed a system of dual morality in regard to

Gentiles, especially in financial dealings, since the Talmud seemed to approve it. And were Jews forbidden under their religious laws to mix freely with non-Jews, eating with them, marrying them or fighting beside them in times of war?

The answers provided by the Assembly were designed to put these persistent doubts to rest. The Jewish delegates stated, for example, that Jewish law in fact did not prohibit intermarriage with non-Jews (except for Egyptians and the Seven Canaanite Nations) and that Jewish tradition permitted Jews to serve in non-Jewish armies, wearing their clothes, eating their food, and drinking their wine.

There was obviously hedging and evasion in these answers. Most Jews must have been surprised to learn that Jewish law did not prohibit intermarriage, for example, or that dietary and other laws could be lifted for Jews serving in the army. Many tangled issues, similarly, were left not only unresolved but scarcely addressed. For example, were Jews denying the *principle* of civil and human equality in the Enlightened sense by excluding the possibility of marrying Egyptians or members of the Seven Canaanite Nations (who were presumably human)? Should national or tribal identities based on conditions thousands of years in the past continue to regulate the lives of modern people?

On the other hand, the pressures on the Assembly to come up with 'correct' answers were intense, since 'incorrect' answers would certainly have endangered Jewish civil equality, by this time accepted as desirable even by many religious leaders, in western Europe at least. Napoleon's observers at the meetings of the Assembly seemed themselves not much concerned about such awkward points; they described the delegates to the Assembly as 'highly admirable,' so different from 'the dregs' of the Jewish people who had been the cause of the many complaints to French officials up to this point [94 *p. 149*].

But unresolved issues of a fundamental sort lingered, bubbling over at various points throughout the century. Most obviously – and it was a question that dated back to the time of Antiochus Epiphanes – could *halakha*, traditional Jewish law, be reconciled with Enlightened universalism? Following Mendelssohn's lead, highly learned and ingenious efforts would be undertaken by a number of Jewish thinkers in the next few decades to suggest ways that such an apparent squaring of the circle could be accomplished, either by reinterpreting Jewish tradition, or by a fundamental reform of Jewish religious practices. But traditional Jewish leaders were outraged. Far from viewing Napoleon as a liberator, they considered him to be a man of great evil. And as far as traditional Jews were concerned, especially those in eastern Europe, Jews who accepted French law over Jewish law were little better than heretics, traitors to their people and their tradition.

THE GROWING DIFFERENCES OF THE JEWS OF EASTERN AND WESTERN EUROPE

The principles agreed upon in Napoleon's consultation with the Assembly of Jewish Notables were the ones to prevail in France and most of western and central Europe for the rest of the century. Breaking with millennia-old Jewish traditions, Jewish religion and Jewish national identity were indeed separated; modern Jews came to insist on being called Frenchmen, Germans or Italians of Jewish religion, rather than members of the Jewish nation living in France, Germany, or Italy. In a parallel way, the earlier doubts about whether Jews would live up to the expectations of citizenship gradually diminished; a majority of French Jews undeniably assimilated into French culture in the course of the nineteenth century. They similarly began to diversify their economic roles, entering the liberal professions, government positions, and even the military in significant numbers by the middle years of the century. The process was broadly similar for much of the rest of western and central Europe, although full civil equality did not come to the Jews in central Europe until after mid-century.

This triumph of the ideals of modern secular nationalism over premodern religious traditions was much slower to come to eastern Europe, particularly to those territories ruled by the Russian tsars. There was thus a fundamental difference in the experience and nature of Europe's Jews in the nineteenth century, a difference that would have far-reaching implications for the evolution of anti-Semitism by the end of the century. The contrast was all the more significant in that eastern Europe was where the vast majority of Europe's Jews lived, roughly three million of them at the beginning of the nineteenth century, which was about 80 percent of those in Europe. Roughly one-hundredth as many Jews lived in France as in the Russian Empire. Moreover, in the course of the nineteenth century the Jewish population of eastern Europe continued the remarkable demographic expansion it had begun in the previous century, in many areas growing far more rapidly than the surrounding non-Jewish population [122 *p. 703*].

Eastern Europeans lived in conditions that were economically undeveloped, closer in most regards to the middle ages than modern times. The industrial revolution that was transforming most of the rest of Europe affected eastern Europe notably less. Low levels of literacy, extreme poverty, and rank superstition were common among both Jews and non-Jews. Literacy was higher among Jews than non-Jews, but illiteracy did exist among the poorest elements of the Jewish population. Much of the Christian peasantry remained enserfed until the 1860s. The political reforms of the French Revolution had been carried to much of central Europe but not to the Slavic regions ruled by the tsars. The issue of giving equal rights to the Jews finally had little meaning in an area where rights in the western sense scarcely existed for anyone, and where the tsar was an absolute autocrat.

When Russia took over most of the Polish commonwealth in the partitions that ended the independent existence of Poland at the end of the eighteenth century, a new time of troubles for the Jews began. The treatment of the Jews by the tsars was not so uniformly horrific as folk memory and some older historical accounts would have it, but there is little question that under Russian rule the Jews faced suspicion, incomprehension, and oppression, whereas they had previously enjoyed centuries of relative toleration and support by Polish kings and nobles.

Up to the time of the partitions, Jews had been forbidden to enter the lands of Holy Russia. Similarly, Russian Orthodox faith retained stronger Judeophobic elements than most other strains of Christianity. In a more general way, Russian national identity had long been marked by paranoia and fears of subversion. That 80 percent of Europe's Jews, including its poorest, most Orthodox, separatist and ethnocentric, should suddenly be incorporated into Europe's most intolerant and xenophobic Christian state did not bode well for the future.

In an effort to limit what the tsars and their officials regarded as a danger of Jewish contamination, the so-called Pale of [Jewish] Settlement was established, an area basically encompassing the lands formerly ruled by the Poles. A stream of special and often inconsistent laws for the Jews was also passed in the course of the century, with the expressed purpose of keeping them under special control. The alleged danger of contamination from Jews was not presented primarily in religious terms, although religious imagery unquestionably reinforced the sense of secular or physical danger. The tsars and their officials regularly expressed concern that the Jews would exploit the peasants economically, through money-lending and related activities, as well as corrupting them morally, through the production and sale of alcohol, which were to an important degree in the hands of Jews.

While the evolution of Jewish–Gentile relations in most of western and central Europe seemed to be working gradually in the direction of mutual understanding and harmony, comparable developments in Russia were at best weak. There was some hope for better times under the reforming tsar, Alexander II, who in the 1860s freed the serfs and loosened restrictions in regard to those Jews deemed to be 'useful,' such as doctors and large-scale merchants. But the reforming years came to a shattering end with Alexander's assassination in 1881, in which some Jews were implicated, as they had been in a number of terrorist acts and attacks on tsarist officials in the years immediately before 1881. Fear of Jewish subversion escalated.

The 1880s marked a souring of Jewish–Gentile relations in both western and central Europe, which will be the main subject of the following chapter; here the main point is the difference between the two areas before then. In Russia, mutual suspicion and separatism were the prevalent themes from the beginning of the century; in western and central Europe an incomparably greater mutual *rapprochement* of Jew and non-Jew under conditions of civil equality, or major steps in that direction, prevailed. The older Jewish sense of cultural superiority persisted in eastern Europe but had slipped badly by the 1870s in much of the rest of Europe. Modern western civilization exercised powerful attractions for Jews, to the extent of undermining a sense of the worth of remaining Jewish for large numbers of them. Not only did many Jews embrace Gentile ways – language, dress, nationality – but they often expressed feelings of embarrassment and even revulsion for those Jews who remained traditional.

Eastern Jews were described by western Jews as primitive, superstitious, and malodorous. Western Jews, according to those from the east, were stiff, supercilious, and cold, but more important, eastern Jews charged that western Jews had made an appalling mistake in embracing the ways of the *goyim*. The exchanges were perhaps the ugliest between German Jews and *Ostjuden* (the somewhat contemptuous German term for eastern Jew), played out on many levels. German Jews, for example, prided themselves in speaking high German, the precise and noble language of Kant and Goethe, whereas the *Ostjuden* spoke Yiddish, which German Jews considered a nasal, whining, and crippled ghetto jargon.

RACE AND 'SCIENTIFIC' RACISM IN NINETEENTH-
CENTURY EUROPE

Such invidious cultural hierarchies were commonly embraced in the nineteenth century, among non-Jews as well as Jews. The English, French, and Germans particularly thought of themselves as superior, more advanced and civilized, than the peoples of eastern and southern Europe. Such attitudes had deep roots in European civilization but grew in importance as western European science outpaced that of the rest of the world and as the industrial revolution helped European powers to gain control over whole continents outside Europe.

Feelings of cultural superiority, couched in a vocabulary that might be loosely termed 'racist,' have characterized many civilizations. Aristotle, the great philosopher of ancient Greece, believed that the peoples who later became English, French and German were inherently slow in mental processes. The Chinese thought of the Europeans as descended from monkeys and remaining like them. An Arab sage of the eleventh century thought of Europeans as spiritually cold and inherently lacking in intellectual quickness, while another prominent Arab intellectual wrote disparagingly of the cultural traits of black Africans and their 'proximity to the animal stage' [108 *p. 72*].

But European racism, deeming itself 'scientific' in the nineteenth century, made both more precise and more sweeping claims. The belief in cultural hierarchies came to be increasingly linked to a belief that body type and intellectual proclivity had some sort of inner or inherent 'racial' unity. By later and more rigorous definitions of science, much of this theorizing must be dismissed as little more than imaginative and highly fallible speculation, but it was widely accepted as scientific at the time. By the end of the nineteenth century, a belief in the role of race in determining cultural accomplishment or 'civilization' was widespread among the literate population of most advanced European nations.

Some sense of the imprecision as well as the psychological allure of racial theory can be gained by a look at a few of the most influential writers on race in mid-century. Of those who began to use a vocabulary of racial determinism, Ernst Renan was one of the most widely read. By the 1850s he was using the term 'Semite' to refer not only to the Jews but to other peoples of the Middle East who spoke Semitic languages, such as the Arabs, and who had similar cultural traits, notably intolerance and a lack of openness to change. The Jews, in their Semitic single-mindedness, had brought ethical monotheism to the world, a precious advance in civilization at the time,

Renan believed, but they were then unable to evolve further; their self-imposed isolation and cultural sterility were frozen in place by talmudic thought.

In spite of such theories, Renan maintained friendly contacts with contemporary Jews, among whom he found many admirers. He was also capable of changing his mind when faced with new evidence; later in his life, he moved away from some of his generalizations about Semitic traits, in part because he was repelled by the anti-Semitic movements that were putting his theories to uses he had not intended. Personally, he harbored no doubts that modern Jews could embrace other identities voluntarily; their Semitic race did not prevent them from becoming modern citizens.

By this time a belief in racial determinism seemed to be spreading and seeping down into the general population. Indeed, even among those who argued for the primary role of environment in determining character, many accepted generalizations about how race also played a role. Jews themselves joined in this general consensus. To say that one was 'Jewish by race but not religion' was one convenient way for an assimilated Jew to describe his or her identity, recognizing certain different physical and psychological traits within a general identity as a member of a modern nation state. Contrary to the situation in the late twentieth century, there seems to have been a growing consensus among Jews and non-Jews alike that Jews constituted a race, the Semitic race. Indeed, Jews were often believed to constitute an unusually clear example of a 'pure' race because of Judaism's strictures against intermarriage.

Racial thinking of this sort easily blended into pre-existing negative imagery about Jews as devious, intolerant, and destructive. But such negative images were somewhat less widespread in the nineteenth century than they had been in the past. Assimilated Jews not only found acceptance and moved up the economic and social scales; they were given many signs of public esteem, of a sort that would have been unimaginable a century before.

One such widely esteemed Jew might be considered the most prominent and influential of all proponents in the nineteenth century of the significance of racial determinants. Benjamin Disraeli, British prime minister in 1868 and then from 1874 to 1880, let it be known that although he had been brought up as a Christian, he remained a proud member of the Jewish race (and of the especially race-conscious Sephardim). Jews, he observed, had exercised a clandestine power throughout history by cooperating across national borders to forward collective Jewish interests. In one of his novels, *Coningsby*, the noble

Jewish character, Sidonia, exclaims 'all is race. There is no other truth;' western civilization would not have been possible without the contributions of the Jewish race [108 *pp. 76–7*].

How many contemporaries fully accepted Disraeli's claims – which had a transparent element of exaggerated boasting in order to counter negative images of the Jews – is difficult to determine, but he would often be quoted by anti-Semites in confirmation of their charges of clannish and clandestine Jewish power. Most British leaders seemed to consider Disraeli an odd character, not really English, if still an asset to the country. He was particularly liked by Queen Victoria, whom he assiduously flattered.

Friedrich Nietzsche, widely considered by scholars to be one of the most influential writers of the nineteenth century, made pronouncements about the Jews that resembled those of Disraeli. He regarded the Jews as the 'strongest, toughest, and purest race now living in Europe,' and he also shared Disraeli's sense of how powerful the Jews could be, or had been [88 *p. 377*]. His example further underlines a point that is easily missed: racial thinking took on bewilderingly diverse forms, not always negative in regard to Jews. Renan had critical things to say about the Semites in history but he also praised them and rejected modern political anti-Semitism. Disraeli, who was inclined to unbounded glorification of the role of Jews in history, was used by anti-Semites to verify their own negative assertions about Jews. Nietzsche's case is even more complicated, in part because his writings were so subtle and elusive. The Nazis later cut snippets from his writings to support their own crude social darwinism and racism, but there is little question that he would have been even more repelled by the Nazis than he was by the anti-Semites of his day.

Generalizations among the general population about Jews as a race in the nineteenth century remained a mix of negative and positive. Even commonly held views (for example, that Jews were clannish or had too much economic power) did not necessarily result in a strong hostility to all Jews, so long as those views were matched by others that stressed the usefulness or decency of some Jews. In short, a widespread belief in 'Semitism' – a cluster of inherent traits in the Jewish race – did not necessarily lead to anti-Semitism.

Revealingly, the most scientific of the racial theorists of the nineteenth century tended to be the least negative in their evaluations of the Jewish race. Some agreed with Disraeli that Jews were one of the superior races; it was often remarked that the very survival of Jews over the centuries gave striking proof of their racial fitness. (The notion of the survival of the fittest human races became widely

accepted in the field of social darwinism, a term derived from Charles
Darwin's influential theories about the survival of species in the
natural world.) Those hostile to Jews as a race were frequently,
though not infallibly, the more mystical thinkers, or the more slip-
shod in their applications of scientific principles.

The writings of the widely recognized 'father of modern racism,'
Count Arthur de Gobineau, further suggest some of the overlooked
intricacies of racist thinking in regard to the Jews in the nineteenth
century. Like Renan, Gobineau was a learned man by the standards
of the mid-century; he also used linguistic evidence to demonstrate the
superiority of the 'Aryans,' a Sanscrit term meaning 'noble' that had
been coined in the earlier part of the century to refer to what today
are termed Indo-European languages. He believed that the upper
classes of Europe were the descendents of Aryan invaders; the upper
classes were everywhere the source of creativity and progress in
civilization.

Gobineau pushed what could be called the essentialist core of
racist thinking to its logical conclusion: environment did not explain
the rise of civilizations but rather inherent racial genius did; the
decline of civilizations was due to the dilution of that genius through
race mixing. The phrase in Disraeli's novel, 'all is race; there is no
other truth,' was thus consistent with Gobineau's theories. Revealingly,
Gobineau considered the Jews to be one of the superior 'white' races
and approved of their efforts throughout history to remain racially
pure. He made more hostile remarks about the Jews later in his life, once
he made contact with anti-Semitic circles in Germany, where his racist
theories attracted more favorable attention than in his native France.

Gobineau's racism was widely criticized, especially in his own
country, but in one revealing regard it was widely accepted both in
Europe and among people of European descent in the Americas:
African Blacks were, he asserted, a distinctly inferior race. For
Gobineau, Africans and the European lower orders had common
traits – low intelligence, lack of self-control, and proclivity to
violence. For all its claims to scientific validity, this view had deep
roots in the European and Judeo-Christian past, going back to texts
of the Bible as well as commentary on it. Indeed, the terminology of
modern racial theory derived from biblical mythology in the account
of Noah and his sons (Gen., 9:21–27): Shem, from whom the Semites
descended; Ham, from whom the African Hamites descended; and
Japheth, from whom the Europeans descended.

Those Christians who sought to defend slavery as divinely sanctioned drew upon biblical texts, although many leading Christian

spokesmen opposed the enslavement of Africans. Some rabbinical commentary also contained proto-racist elements, enhancing for example the derogation of Blacks more than the bare biblical text in making the sons of Ham 'ugly and dark-skinned' [47 *p. 32*; 108 *p. 72*]. The influential Jewish medieval philosopher Moses Maimonides wrote that 'the Blacks' nature. ... is below that of man and above that of a monkey' [159 *p. 25*]. So Disraeli might be said to have drawn from both modern scientific and age-old sources when he concluded that if the white population of the United States were to continue to 'mingle with [its] negro and coloured population', an inevitable degeneration of the civilization of the young republic would be the result [18 *p. 275*].

Negative beliefs about Blacks as a race, then, had stronger roots and were more widely embraced than were negative beliefs about Jews as a race. More precisely, there was a different range and quality of beliefs about Jews. Blacks were often described as lacking in intelligence, Jews as cunning, dangerously intelligent. Blacks allegedly lacked self-control, whereas Jews were seen as disciplined and devious. Insofar as Jews were described as inferior, it usually had to do with moral issues, although their small stature, weak bodies, and odd 'Oriental' appearance were also often mentioned. In short, negative visions of Blacks tended to describe them as animal-like, at a lower stage of evolution; they could be used in the way beasts of burden were used and were dangerous in the way that such animals can be dangerous. But there was no concern in nineteenth-century Europe or America that Blacks were taking over the world through clandestine power and financial manipulation.

It was not so much the weakness of the Jews that fanned hatred of them as a fear of an expanding and malevolent Jewish power. This is not to deny that the alleged inferiority of the Jews was also a source of negative attitudes, but such attitudes came in milder forms (avoidance, social exclusion, derision, for example). Those who feared Jews, above all when they believed Jews had demonic powers and destructive goals, were not surprisingly inclined to more vicious and aggressive forms of hatred. In a number of cases that hatred was expressed by a desire to see Jews driven from the land or even put to death. The issue of Jewish weakness versus Jewish power is by no means simple, however: perceived weakness in Jews undoubtedly whetted criminal appetites in times of trouble; rampaging mobs did not need to believe in the demonic powers of Jews in order to rob them. Similarly, hatred usually came in impenetrably mixed forms; it often seemed that contempt for Jews as weak and servile connected in some sort of twisted, impenetrable dialectic with fear of them as alien and demonically powerful.

Such demonization of the Jews is to be seen in a number of important thinkers in the nineteenth century, strikingly in Pierre-Joseph Proudhon. He was a major theorist of anarchism and in other regards widely influential. Proudhon's hatred of Jews stunningly mixed racial thought and a demonization that borrowed from Christian modes of thought:

> The Jews, unsociable, stubborn, infernal. ... First authors of the malicious superstition called Catholicism. ... Make a prevision against that race – which poisons everything by butting in everywhere without ever merging with any people – to demand its expulsion from France, except for individuals married to French women. Abolish the synagogues. ... The Jew is the enemy of mankind. That race must be sent back to Asia or exterminated. [137, 3 *p. 376*]

Elsewhere Proudhon described the Jew as 'always fraudulent and parasitic, in business and in philosophy. ... He is the evil element, Satan ... incarnate in the race of Shem' [137, 3 *p. 374*].

Another influential racial theorist of the day, Eugen Dühring, was at least as hate-filled as Proudhon. Again his fury was directed against both the Jews and Christianity; he believed the Judeo-Christian tradition represented a 'hatred of life,' a diseased 'slave morality.' He urged a return to pre-Christian, more healthy and natural Germanic beliefs. Jews, he believed, were a cosmic, inhuman force for evil and destruction [108 *pp. 160–1*].

These expressions of extreme hatred of Jews, while having an influence on anti-Semites in the late nineteenth and early twentieth centuries, were not typical of the middle years of the nineteenth century; indeed such hatred remained on the margins even in the more troubled periods of the late nineteenth and early twentieth centuries. Although both Proudhon and Dühring were leftists, it is important to recognize that their peculiar kind of hatred was not typical of the left, that indeed friendly feelings for Jews were prevalent on the left to left-center in Europe. The non-Jew, Franz Mehring, a leading social democrat in Germany, commented that 'side by side with a great many defects in modern Jewry, it is perhaps its highest glory that there is not one person of culture in Germany who is not linked in intimate relations of heart and intellect with one or more Jews' [118 *p. 424*]. Friedrich Engels, also non-Jewish, wrote toward the end of his life: 'We owe a great deal to the Jews. ... [among them are] people of whose friendship I am proud' [118 *p. 312*]. Karl Kautsky, the leading Marxist theoretician after the death of Marx and Engels and also non-Jewish, remarked that 'Jews have given to the world more great thinkers ... perhaps than any nation ...' [108 *p. 172*].

Such admiration was also to be found among the common people: it was said of the Jew, Paul Singer, that 'no one achieved such popularity among the Berlin masses. ... [His] funeral was the most impressive that Berlin had ever seen' [118 *p. 424*]. Jewish figures among leading socialists, at times the object of near mystical adulation by the masses, were fairly common.

Jewish–Gentile friendships were often part of left-wing political activity, looking to reforming state and society; Jews and other 'outsiders,' such as manual laborers, were natural allies. People on the traditionalist right were more often devout Christians and more often retained traditional Christian reservations about Jews in general. In them one often encountered the belief, which could ultimately be traced back to Saint Augustine, that it was improper that Jews should thrive and rise in Christian society. When Jews constituted a prominent element of their left-wing opponents, conservatives were all the more likely to detest them. Nonetheless, friendly contacts between conservatives and Jews were hardly unknown in most countries. The German chancellor, Otto von Bismarck, had a Jewish lawyer, banker, and doctor; he worked closely with a number of converted Jews and appointed other men of Jewish origin to high office. Friendly or intimate contacts, including intermarriage, between members of the British upper classes and Jews were the most notable of any country, but they existed in nearly all.

In conclusion, it should be re-emphasized that although racist ideas had much potential to be anti-Jewish, they could be and were often used by supporters of the Jews as well as by Jews themselves. Similarly, racial stereotypes of a sort that would be roundly condemned today were commonplace in the nineteenth century without apparent evil intent. In the meetings of the German Social-Democratic Party, what appear to modern sensibilities tasteless jokes about Jewish physical traits, noses in particular, were often heard, to the apparent merriment of all, Jews included [108 *p. 173*].

No doubt some small part of the reason that such racist stereotypes were not always considered hostile or were not put to malevolent use is that the middle years of the century were ones of great prosperity and optimism about the future, with few if any parallels in European history. In such an environment, ethnic or racial frictions were taken less seriously. There was a pervasive faith in progress, a sense that the march of reason and scientific progress in all realms would solve age-old problems. Jews and other elements of society who felt mistreated had not only a sense of common cause but a growing confidence that the future was theirs, whatever the current difficulties. Still, these were tenuous matters, even in the 1850s and 1860s. When economic growth seemed to come to a halt in the early 1870s, many suppressed frictions and resentments came to the fore.

3 MODERN RACIAL-POLITICAL ANTI-SEMITISM

The issue of how deep the roots of Nazi anti-Semitism are has been endlessly debated. The efforts of scholars to find the roots of the Holocaust in the middle ages and even farther have been sometimes thought-provoking, often unpersuasive, but there is a wider consensus among scholars that in the late nineteenth century solid roots – more than traces or tendrils – are to be found. These were the years of Hitler's birth; the ideas in the air formed his worldview. Nazi terms such as Aryan, Superman (*Übermensch*) or indeed anti-Semite, were either coined in this period or came to have a wider acceptance in it. Modern forms of extreme nationalism grew more powerful, especially by the turn of the century, mixing into more xenophobic, hate-filled forms of racism, also key traits of National Socialism.

Still, the nature of the various forms of Jew-hatred that appeared in these years is by no means simple and is often misunderstood. The generalization found in many textbooks, that religious hatred was now replaced by racial hatred, has some truth in it but overlooks the important fact that hatred based in religious imagery was still very often expressed. Similarly, much of the hostility directed at Jews in this period was not racial but cultural (granting that the two terms are slippery and overlap). More central to the nature of this new kind of Jew-hatred was the way it embraced an activist program; political movements arose that stepped beyond the kind of intellectual or literary attacks described in the previous chapter and sought to mobilize large masses of people and find concrete political solutions to the Jewish question. These movements were all characterized to some degree by a use of the new vocabulary of race, but modern anti-Semitism remained from beginning to end confused and contradictory. Its proponents differed in fundamental ways, and an often fierce internal factionalism contributed to the general ineffectiveness of the anti-Semitic movements that continually formed and reformed. Insofar as there was a unity of purpose among them it had to do with an alarm about the rise of the Jews, an older issue that took on new urgency in troubled times.

A key point, then, is that the new anti-Semitism not only spoke in political terms but developed in a significantly different economic climate from the boom years of the 1850s and 1860s. What was termed at the time 'the Great Depression' started with stock market crashes in 1873, especially notable in Berlin and Vienna. In the following two decades industrial production in most of the advanced nations faltered, unemployment rose, and agriculture experienced a series of crises. The economic difficulties of these years were in truth mild compared to those of the Great Depression of the 1930s, but they were nonetheless a great shock to those who had expressed such confidence in the free market, economic growth, and continual progress. People who were hurt economically looked for someone to blame.

Resentments focused on Jews for a number of reasons. They were prominent in the stock market in most countries, and Jewish names were linked to many of the financial scandals of the day. But the disproportionate number of Jews involved in publicly exposed wrongdoing was probably not the main issue; rather it was that Jews were now believed to be in positions of growing and decisive importance in the modern nation states of Europe. Exaggerations of that importance naturally connected to long-standing fantasies about Jews and money. Similarly, Jews were closely identified with the free market and such key aspects of modern economic life as railroad building and department stores.

It was hardly surprising that those who were unhappy about these developments were inclined to denounce them as the fault of Jews. Similarly, those who thought of Europe as a Christian civilization were alarmed at the prospect that Jews, who constituted less than one percent of the population in most industrially advanced countries, should rise to play such a prominent role in that civilization. Jewish success in times of prosperity was easier to accept, especially if Jews appeared to have some responsibility for that prosperity. But it inevitably worked both ways, and Jews were blamed when prosperity waned.

By the final decades of the nineteenth century, the rise of the Jews in most industrially advanced nations was indeed impressive in range and texture. The granting of civil equality itself may be seen as a kind of rise, one that served as a foundation or lubricant for other kinds. Demographically, too, there was a palpable Jewish increase. It is reasonably clear that from the mid-eighteenth century until the eve of the Holocaust, the Jewish population of Europe increased faster than that of the non-Jewish population. There was also a more rapid move of Jews than non-Jews into urban areas, especially capital cities, another kind of significant rise in status. Per capita income rose more rapidly among Jews, again in certain areas strikingly so. Even in regions where Jews were known to be desperately poor, they were less poor on average than the surrounding non-Jewish, usually peasant population. The percentage of Jews who were among the very wealthiest citizens of Europe's nation states shot up by the end of the century, as did the number of Jews who won Nobel prizes after 1905. Even where Jews rose rapidly, there remained spheres where they encountered stubborn exclusion, such as the Prussian military or the diplomatic corps in most countries, but overall the record of Jewish success, of social, economic, and even political ascent, is far more impressive than the examples of blocked access, especially considering the pariah status of Jews less than a century before. Change of such speed and dimensions has few parallels in history – and could hardly occur without repercussions.

In the Russian Empire the rise of the Jews was decidedly less clear-cut, the pariah status more widely and crudely retained. It was a major concern of the tsarist government to do what it could to block a Jewish rise in Russia comparable to that in countries to Russia's west. Given the fact that around 80 percent of Europe's Jewish population was concentrated in the western regions of Russia, the prospect of rapidly rising Jews was cause for special alarm in the country's ruling circles. In a related way, the far-reaching liberalization that western states had introduced was considered unattractive, impossible even, given the character of the Russian population and the country's autocratic traditions.

An English observer who had spent much time in Russia in the 1890s dealing with the officials of the tsar summed up their apprehensions by stating that if Russia were to 'fling down the barriers to Jewish emancipation ... in ten years every place of importance in the empire would be filled by a Jew' [163 *p. 153*]. An influential Russian minister openly stated that the Jews were natively more intelligent and enterprising than the Slavic population. A strong government supervision of the Jews was necessary to protect the rest of the population from Jewish predatory traits; without state protection the ignorant and gullible peasants would soon become little more than slaves to the Jews, especially since many Jews encouraged drunkenness and improvidence among the peasants by selling them vodka, then getting them into debt, and finally taking over their lands and other possessions [108 *p. 282*].

From 1820 to 1880, Jewish numbers grew about 150 percent, compared to 87 percent for non-Jews [*12 pp. 63–4*]. Unprecedented population growth characterized most of Europe in modern times. The 1840s, 'the hungry forties,' in particular had witnessed some of the tragic implications of very rapid population growth. The famine in Ireland was only the most notorious of many horrific episodes, with millions dead and millions more uprooted, fanning a hostility between the Irish and their British overlords that was no less intense than the hostility of Jews to their Russian overlords.

TSARIST RUSSIA AND THE DILEMMAS OF MODERNIZATION

Gradually but very painfully, the industrial revolution helped to feed, clothe, and house these new millions, but industrialization was late in coming to Russia. To some degree population pressures were relieved by movement to the less densely populated regions of the south and Siberian east. Nonetheless, malnutrition, class conflict, crowded slums, crime, and ethnic strife in Russia were even more serious than in the rest of Europe. The situation in the Russian Empire was made no better by the pervasive incompetence and corruption of tsarist officials. Emigration to the New World was another major way to release pressure. It was a solution that came to have growing allures for Russia's leaders, especially in dealing with their perplexing Jewish population. By the late 1870s a confluence of factors began to come together to facilitate and accelerate emigration, including available transport, countries of destination with a labor shortage, and the effects of the Great Depression.

Russia's leaders could not seal the country off from modernizing influences. The desire to keep out western ideas clashed with a growing recognition that modernization in the west was allowing potential enemies, such as Britain, Germany, and France, to become steadily more powerful in a military sense. The above-described modernizing reforms of Alexander II in the 1860s reflected that worried recognition. Prominent among the unwelcome imports were western liberal-democratic and revolutionary ideas. Elements of Russia's intellectual elites began to embrace visions of revolutionary redemption. Anarchist 'propaganda of the deed,' as assassinations and other acts of terror were called, came to be seen as answers to

Russia's problems: by killing the officials of the tsar, or even the tsar himself, revolutionaries believed they could demonstrate both their own power and the hollow claims of the authorities to rule. An act of violence would expose the tsarist regime as rotten, unable to defend itself, inspiring a mass uprising and the installation of a new regime of reason and justice.

Western revolutionary theories attracted almost no following among Jews in the early to middle years of the century, but as the century progressed the ranks of both Jewish and non-Jewish revolutionaries grew. Whether the growth was faster among Jews than non-Jews is uncertain; tsarist officials certainly believed the Jewish revolutionary to be especially dangerous. The image of the fanatically destructive Jewish revolutionary would at any rate come to play a major role in nearly all countries.

The issue of Jews in revolutionary opposition to the tsar was much complicated by the anti-Jewish riots, or pogroms, that erupted after the tsar was murdered in 1881. There was a widespread belief at the time and for many years after that the pogroms had been actively encouraged by the authorities. However, recent careful studies have provided a less simple and more plausible picture. The new tsar, Alexander III, was himself taken aback by the riots and assumed that they were part of a general agitation against tsarist rule. Popular rioting of this sort had long been a nightmare of the tsars; rousing the ignorant and anarchic 'black masses' was not something the authorities would be likely to do. A commission set up by Alexander III to study the cause of the unrest concluded that the pogroms reflected peasant resentment against increased Jewish exploitation under the liberalization of the previous decades.

That conclusion resembled the one in the complaints to Napoleon that Jews liberated under the new French constitution had used their liberties to exploit more efficiently. In Russia, it was only too predictable, since conservatives had long warned about the dangers of reform. The actual origins and nature of the riots were less simple than peasant resentment against Jewish exploitation, although the riots undoubtedly had in part to do with fears and jealousies about rising Jews. However, it seems that it was less the peasant masses than other parts of the population, including non-Jewish merchants, artisans, and professionals, who played key roles; there is suggestive evidence that although some peasants resented or feared Jewish enterprise, many others welcomed it. In some areas peasants were known to have protected Jews from the rioters. Some peasants who had opportunistically participated in the looting showed contrition afterwards, returning items they had stolen and asking forgiveness from their Jewish neighbors [7 *p. 29*; 108 *p. 69*].

The new controls introduced in the so-called May Laws of 1882 included a stricter limitation on Jewish movement out of the Pale of Jewish Settlement to other parts of the Russian Empire, restrictions on ownership and leasing of land by Jews outside urban areas, and quotas of around 10 percent on the numbers of Jews allowed to attend schools of higher education. Although the proclaimed rationale of the Laws was to protect the peasantry from the Jews and to preserve social peace for the Jews' own good, the Laws added palpably to the long-standing sense of grievance that most Jews felt toward the tsarist authorities. And that sense provided yet another reason to want to get out of the country, which seemed ever more mired in suspicion, incompetence, and corruption.

In the next four decades more than three million Jews left Russia, one of the most remarkable migrations of people in history. That they left in the hundreds of thousands from other poverty-stricken areas of eastern Europe, principally Galicia (a province of the Austro-Hungarian Empire) and Romania, suggests that the pogroms and May Laws were finally not the main driving force behind emigration from Russia. In Galicia, Jews enjoyed civil equality and an emperor, Franz Joseph, who was far more benevolent in their regard than any tsar. Galician Jews experienced no pogroms, but they nonetheless emigrated in roughly the same proportions as the Jews of Russia. The main issues motivating them, in short, seem to have been that they were as poor as Russian Jews, felt the similar population pressures, and dreamed of enjoying a more secure material life.

These emigrants passed through and sometimes lingered in other parts of Europe before leaving for the New World. The prospect that millions of poverty-stricken Jews might actually settle in the countries of western Europe added significantly to the anti-Jewish agitation of these depression years. The small numbers of eastern European Jews who did indeed remain in Germany, France, or Britain were, given their characteristic clothing and culture, highly visible and often perceived as alien. For such reasons overheated warnings about the threats they allegedly posed were often given credence. It is of no small significance that a defining moment in Hitler's own evolving anti-Semitism came, at least by his own retrospective account, in an encounter with an eastern European Jew in Vienna. In *Mein Kampf* he described having 'suddenly encountered an apparition in black caftan and black hairlocks ... [with] foreign face ... [and] unheroic appearance.' The Inner City of Vienna, he lamented, 'swarmed with people' who obviously were not Germans. Their filth was unbearable. He wrote that 'I often grew sick to my stomach from the smell of these caftan wearers.' The passages immediately following this description are among the most shrill and full of hate in all of *Mein Kampf*: 'Was there any form of filth or profligacy ... without at least one Jew in it?' [*74 pp. 56-8; Doc. 16*].

In fact, a large proportion of the Jews of Vienna by the time Hitler lived there (1908–13) had abandoned the most visible signs of their Jewishness and had adopted German language and culture. They were rising rapidly in wealth and social position. Their numerical rise was particularly striking: from 6,000 in 1860 to 175,000 in 1910, an increase of around thirty times within two generations. Budapest, the other capital of the Dual Monarchy, experienced an even more precipitous increase in the same years, resulting in a Jewish percentage of 23 percent by 1914, compared to Vienna's 9 percent [*59 p. 77; 108 pp. 188–9; 146 p. 18*].

THE RISE OF GERMANY AND GERMANY'S 'SPECIAL' ANTI-SEMITISM

The rise of the Jews in the new German Empire was more gradual than in Austria and Hungary. Berlin's Jewish population was around 5 percent by the turn of the century, its growth slower over the course of the century [*122 p. 708*], but most histories of modern anti-Semitism have given special place to Germany in the 1870s and 1880s. The quality of that attention has obviously had much to do with the later horrors of Nazism, but even at the time German anti-Semitism attracted special notice Europe-wide.

One reason that anti-Semitism erupted with such force in Germany was that the Great Depression was a special shock for the German population. But the attention of other countries to Germany at this time had probably more to do with German successes than its economic difficulties. In 1870–71 Prussian-led Germany had defeated France, and many believed that the Germans were destined to replace the French as the dominant people on the Continent. Well before that dazzling victory over France, German scientists, scholars, and artists had been attracting growing admiration throughout the world. Germans were regarded not only as an unusually disciplined people but as supremely cultivated Europeans; German achievements were seen as a triumph of European civilization. What could it mean that such a country seemed to be turning against its Jewish citizens?

The 'German problem' had been a topic of discussion for most of the century; its 'solution' under Prussian leadership left Germany's neighbors uneasy – even those who had not been humiliated in the battlefield. Revealingly, the German problem and the Jewish problem, for all their differences, were perceived as having certain common traits. Both Jews and Germans rapidly were rising (in numbers, wealth, esteem, power) in ways that challenged the status quo; both had learned unusually well how to tap modern trends; both displayed the peculiar mix of brashness, arrogance, and insecurity of the former underdog. In short, both Germans and Jews were viewed with a volatile mix of admiration and aversion.

Jew-hatred in Russia, whether from the government or the people, was no surprise, but for anti-Semitism to become such an issue in Germany was seen as far more significant – and troubling. Hostility to Jews in German-speaking lands of course existed before the 1870s, but in fact Germans did not have, by the late nineteenth century, the reputation for Jew-hatred that they would later acquire. The expressions of friendship and esteem for Jews quoted in the previous chapter came from Germans, and those expressions were not unrepresentative. It would be easy to cite comparable examples of philo-Semitism in other countries, Britain in particular, but almost certainly not in greater numbers, or by more influential figures. Jews in German lands were, at any rate, around ten times more numerous than in Britain, and the interplay of Jew and non-Jew was more remarkable in German-speaking lands than in the English-speaking ones. In some elusive but potent way, that interplay unleashed genius of simply spectacular dimensions. Any list of the most famous and influential intellects of European civilization between the French Revolution and the Nazi takeover would contain a strongly disproportionate number of German Jews, among them Marx, Freud, and Einstein. But aside from these superstars, as it were, there were hundreds and thousands of German Jews of outstanding accomplishments.

Similarly, whether among great intellects or ordinary citizens, the Jewish embrace of German culture in the course of the nineteenth century was among the most thorough and enthusiastic of any in the world. So too was German–Jewish patriotism. 'German Jew' in a cultural and linguistic sense, however, was a much broader category than Jews who lived in the newly unified German Reich; outside that Reich Jewish love of things German was more cultural than political and nationalistic. Hundreds of thousands of German-speaking Jews, part of the 'German cultural realm' (*deutscher Kulturbereich*), lived in the Austro-Hungarian Empire, as well as in Switzerland and indeed in the Balkans and in the Russian Empire, often in distinct ethnic pockets. For such German Jews the intense patriotism expressed by Jews living in the German Reich was hardly an option. German-speaking Jews residing outside the Reich also usually had more immediate connections to Orthodox backgrounds, fewer contacts with non-Jews, and stronger feelings of Jewish ethnic and national identity. Anti-Semitism directed at such Jews, similarly, could be seen as different in nature from that directed at Jews in the Reich; it was more plausibly linked to 'normal' tensions between groups with substantially different identities and social positions. The ostensibly irrational or baseless quality of the hostility to assimilated, highly patriotic German Jews in the German Reich was, then, a more troubling phenomenon, more of a surprise – and an affront to those who believed in steady, inevitable progress toward mutual toleration and the end of Jew-hatred.

WILHELM MARR, THE 'PATRIARCH OF ANTI-SEMITISM'

On the other hand, as far as most German anti-Semites were concerned, the reasons for their hostility were not only obvious but based on sound, even 'scientific' reasoning; their positions were not derived from Christian bigotry but legitimate indignation over real issues. Such was notably the case for the figure who has been called 'the patriarch of anti-Semitism,' Wilhelm Marr, a journalist who has usually been credited with coining the term anti-Semite and introducing it to general use. His book, *The Victory of the Jews over the Germans* (1879) became the first anti-Semitic best-seller.

There was much about Marr's thought that did not fit into older anti-Jewish categories, both in terms of the arguments he made publicly and in his own private life. He spoke in his book of having had over the years many friendships and other close contacts with Jews, but he did not mention that three of his four marriages had been to Jewish women or that he had had a son by one of them, making him the father of a Jew according to traditional Jewish law. Thirty years earlier he had been attacked for his alleged philo-Semitism and was believed by some to be Jewish himself. Adding further complication to his case, by the 1890s he broke with the anti-Semitic movement he had done so much to inspire, asking that Jews pardon him for his writings. Even this book, with its angry, ugly passages, contains some disorienting praise for Jews. These paradoxes were symptomatic of the anti-Jewish movements of the late nineteenth and early twentieth centuries.

Marr's description of how the Jews had triumphed over the Germans contained little that was novel, except perhaps its tone of resignation, ostensibly more a rhetorical device than a genuine attitude, although this was a low point in Marr's long life, and his personal depression may have had a bearing on the way he presented his thoughts. He was a middle-brow journalist, not a scholar or original thinker; his writings are best seen as evidence of the filtering down to a broader public of the ideas of more original theorists. Indeed, he himself had written similar things in the 1860s, but they went relatively unnoticed. The decisive element, then, was not so much what Marr said as when he said it. His book struck a chord because of the economic difficulties and other tensions in German society, some of which were related to the rise of the Jews.

A key assertion of the pamphlet was that Semitic racial traits determined Jewish character, which was materialistic and scheming. More to the point, 'Semitism' clashed with and undermined Germanism, which was idealistic and generous. At the same time Marr emphatically distanced himself from Christian myths about the Jews, as from religion generally. He wrote that to blame Jews for deicide was absurd, unworthy of modern civilized thought, and it was ludicrous to charge them with needing Christian blood for Passover. Marr expressed sympathy for Jews who had suffered from Christian persecution over the centuries. He had absolutely no sympathy, on the other hand, for Jewish religion – based, in his words, on a 'business deal' with God [108 *p. 128*; 115 *p. 16*]. When Jews were legitimately disliked, it was not because of groundless or metaphysical fantasies about them but because of quite palpable Jewish traits, among them their 'abhorrence for real work' and their proclivity to exploit the labor of others. These traits were in turn related to Jewish contempt for non-Jews and feelings of superiority to them.

These notions were related to the ideas of *philosophes* like Voltaire, but Marr added racial and social-darwinistic elements, among them the charge that Jews exploit liberal environments to rise to domination of those around them. In short, what Marr claimed to be modern, scientific anti-Semitism had much in common with the Jew-hatred in Russia, the most reactionary nation in Europe. And he seemed aware of that connection; he noted that it was too late for Germany to shake off Jewish domination, but he speculated that perhaps the Slavs would yet succeed. Still, he spoke of a 'brutal anti-Jewish explosion' that was looming in Germany. He soon composed a pamphlet with a more activist stance: *Elect No Jews! The Way to the Victory of Germans over Jewry.*

'RESPECTABLE' ANTI-SEMITISM

Marr's book and political activity were at first dismissed by many observers, including Jews, as mere demagogy – beneath contempt, laughable even. However, when one of Germany's most respected intellectuals, the noted historian and popular university professor, Heinrich von Treitschke, began in late 1879 to publish a series of articles that also expressed indignation about the negative role of Jews in Germany, a wider and more educated audience was drawn into the fray [*Doc. 11*]. Treitschke's attacks were relatively muted; he did not speak of a Jewish 'victory' but of another sort of 'rise,' what he described as the impudence and arrogance of newly influential Jews in Germany, their tendency to destructive criticism and brazen ridicule of Germanic ideals. And in the same few years yet wider attention was given to the issue of newly aggressive Jews, when another respected figure, Adolf Stoecker, the chaplain to the court of the Kaiser, formulated his own denunciations of Jews 'out of control' in a liberal environment and recklessly destructive in their mockery of German Christians.

German Jews who believed that they had abandoned the nationalistic element of traditional Judaism and had identified wholeheartedly with German culture and nationhood found these charges both unfair and shocking. They did not deny that some prominent Jews had said things that were highly offensive to men like Treitschke and Stoecker, but they did not consider such Jews to be representative; Treitschke and Stoecker were over-reacting, or worse, pandering to low hatreds in a period of national crisis.

Interestingly, Franz Mehring, who had expressed his belief that 'there is not one person of culture in Germany who is not linked in intimate relations of heart and intellect with one or more Jews,' expressed agreement with both Treitschke's articles and the replies of prominent Jewish intellectuals to them, finding them both dignified and high-minded. Mehring concurred that the Jewish rise in Germany had its unpleasant aspects: 'In Berlin particularly the Jewish voice in public life reached such a pitch as to make even the most intrepid admirers of the wise Nathan feel ill at ease' [118 *p. 188*]. It is tempting to conclude that if this sort of exchange had been the prevalent kind, the perceived differences between Jews and non-Jews might have been worked out more effectively. Such public discussions were after all the sort that liberals believed would lead to peaceable resolution of problems. Significantly, Treitschke's articles did not call for political measures against Jews; he did not suggest that Jews be stripped of civil rights, nor did he agree with Marr that Jews had a racial essence that was incompatible with becoming 'genuinely' German. Least of all did Treitschke suggest that violent action against Jews was justified.

But what Mehring considered dignified and high-minded seems to have been perceived by others, including some of Treitschke's students, as giving a respectable blessing to distinctly hate-filled initiatives and actions. Stoecker, at any rate, was more tempted by demagogy. Treitschke's attacks remained hortatory – urging Jews to refrain from destructive criticism – but Stoecker entered the fray with inflammatory public speeches and political designs. He hoped in particular to reach the masses of German workers who were straying from Christianity, and so he established a new political party, the Christian Social Workers' Party. However, he soon discovered that his most admiring audiences came from the lower-middle class (*Mittelstand*) rather than manual workers.

Stoecker's main professed concern was the socially destructive impact of industrialization in Germany, what was then called 'the social question.' He believed that the negative aspects of the modern industrial system had much to do with the role of Jews in it. He picked up a slogan that would be central to modern anti-Semitism: 'The social question is the Jewish question.' The impact of the modern Jew was to undermine existing society and hallowed traditions; the Christian sense of social responsibility and community were being weakened by a small but rising and highly influential minority of the population, one that was coming to exercise great power because of its control of the press and crucial aspects of the economy.

Although Treitschke and Stoecker have been described as precursors to Nazism, there were many fundamental differences between them and Hitler. Similarly, Marr was not a charismatic leader in the manner of the later German Führer. Treitschke recognized 'the great number of Jews' who were 'Germans in the best sense' [108 *p. 132*; 174 *p. 40ff.*]. Stoecker warned against hatred and declared that 'we respect Jews as our fellow citizens and honor Judaism as a lower stage of divine revelation' [108 *p. 143*; 174 *p. 251*]. Jews were not in his eyes so racially different as to be permanently alien; Jewish converts to Christianity were welcome. All three men met severe criticism from respectable society for their attacks on Jews. Marr was ridiculed and considered dangerous by many conservatives. Even Stoecker was viewed with suspicion by conservatives, including Bismarck. Many of Treitschke's colleagues distanced themselves from him.

THE BERLIN MOVEMENT, ANTI-SEMITES' PETITION, 'PEASANT KING'

On the other hand, there were figures and movements in these years that may be considered more substantially proto-Nazi, although they remained on the fringes. Houston Stewart Chamberlain, who would become at the turn of the century a far more prestigious and best-selling anti-Semitic author than Marr, quipped that his attendance at the meetings of the political anti-Semites of the 1880s left him 'full of pity and love for all Jews,' so repelled was he by the low-brow tone of the speakers at those meetings [49 *p. 90*].

Berlin was one of the centers of this agitation, but it is revealing that the radical anti-Semites who took part in the so-called Berlin Movement attracted only a small following; the city remained a stronghold of the left liberals, who were firmly opposed to anti-Semitism, indeed many of whose elected leaders were themselves Jews. One of the main accomplishments of the anti-Semites in these years was the circulation of the Anti-Semites' Petition, which gathered some 250,000 signatures and was presented to Bismarck in 1881. The Petition used the new racist language:

> *What future is left to our fatherland if the Semitic element is allowed to make a conquest of our home ground?* ... This tribe, to whom our humane legislation extended the rights of hospitality and the rights of the native, stands further from us in thought and feeling than any other people in the entire Aryan world. [106 *p. 126*]

Nonetheless, its authors remained respectful of existing authority. The anti-Jewish measures they specifically proposed included a request that 'the immigration of alien Jews be at least limited,' that Jews be excluded from high government positions, and that 'the Christian character of the primary school ... be protected' by excluding Jews as teachers in them. The Petition asked, in short, for legal, parliamentary measures, not violent revolutionary action. At any rate, it got nowhere; even such limited anti-Jewish proposals had no chance of winning majority support in the Reichstag. Bismarck finally let it be known that 'I most decidedly disapprove of this fight against the Jews' [108 *p. 148*; 170 *p. 527*].

In many regards more impressive than the Berlin Movement or the Anti-Semites' Petition were the efforts of a man who came to be acclaimed as 'the Peasant King,' Otto Böckel. Young, handsome, and talented, he was elected by a strong majority to the Reichstag in 1887.

During his many excursions into the countryside of Hesse (in central Germany), he was drawn to the plight of the peasants he encountered. He composed a pamphlet that went through a hundred editions in the following two decades: *The Jews, Kings of our Time.* In it he wrote that 'the image of the peasant robbed by the Jew drives me onward' [106 *p. 43*]. By his account, he had attended the trial of a peasant charged with killing a Jew who had allegedly deceived him and taken over his farm. The trial galvanized Böckel to action.

The old theme, then, of the peasant being tricked, exploited, and ruined by the Jew retained power even in rapidly modernizing Germany. There was much about Böckel's activity, indeed, that was emphatically modern as well as backward-looking. He developed spectacle and fanfare, torchlight rallies and parades, music and slogans, skillfully combining traditional peasant festivals with modern political devices. In so doing he not only won an ardent enthusiasm among the peasants but attracted idealistic university students who also believed they could aid the peasants by protecting them from the Jews.

But before too long, this thriving form of political Jew-hatred also began to show signs of inner conflict. Böckel was more of a leftist and genuine social reformer than most anti-Semites; he opposed military expenditures because they so heavily relied on taxing the peasants. He similarly attacked the Junker aristocracy, in part because he believed its members had established connections with Jewish financial magnates. These positions involved him in ever-growing factionalism. His movement, too, became mired in corruption and scandal, finally fizzling, although the peasants continued to revere Böckel for many years afterward.

In examining the depressed 1880s for the roots of Nazism, one can easily see much that plausibly fits, but one major difference is that the strands of anti-Jewish protest did not even come close to unity. For the most part the story of German political anti-Semitism from the 1880s up to 1914 is one of marginality and ignominious decline. Similarly, this wave of anti-Semitism was more respectful of existing authority than that later espoused by Hitler. Another crucial difference was that Germany in the 1880s was far less in crisis than it would be in the early 1930s. Finally, and most importantly, the German anti-Semites of the 1880s operated for the most part within a sense of moral limits, recognizing both the legal and human rights of Jews.

THE BELLE EPOQUE: 1890–1914

By the early 1890s, Europe began to pull out of the depression, and in the next two decades Europe's economy grew once again at a gratifying rate. That economic recovery probably best explains the decline of political anti-Semitism in Germany. It was not the case, however, that these were tranquil years in Europe as a whole; national tensions grew and war clouds loomed. Similarly, other countries before World War I were not so free of violent expressions of anti-Semitism as Germany. Mob violence and political agitation against Jews continued to characterize much of central and eastern Europe, with particularly strong outbursts in the decade spanning the turn of the century.

The most influential of those outbursts occurred in an unexpected place, republican France, where many had assumed that the Jewish question was well on its way to solution. France was widely seen as a leader of western civilization, and Jews no less than non-Jews in other countries looked to France as a beacon of civilized values, the country of the revolution, left-leaning, tolerant, and progressive. As with Germany in the late 1870s and early 1880s, the eruption of anti-Semitism in France, then, was a special shock because of where it occurred. The Dreyfus Affair in France, beginning with the arrest in 1894 of the Jewish Captain Alfred Dreyfus, charged with being a spy for Germany, is often seen as a watershed in the history of modern anti-Semitism. For over a century it has continued to fascinate historians and passionately divide the French nation.

Dreyfus's position as an up-and-coming young officer underlines an important difference between France and Germany. Although Jews were approximately ten times more numerous in Germany than in France, no Jew had risen anywhere near so high in the German military. And contrary to what is often stated, Dreyfus's position was not exceptional; Jews were significantly over-represented in the French military, as they were in other branches of the French state. Jews in France as in Germany were mostly left-wing, but again there was a major difference in that the German state remained monarchist, controlled by conservative interests, whereas France was a republic in which the political center of gravity was moving to the left. In France as elsewhere, it seemed axiomatic that the left was friendly territory for the Jews, the right unfriendly, and thus such a left-leaning republic was ostensibly 'good for the Jews.'

Certainly the rise of the Jews in France was comparable to that in other western countries. By the early 1890s French Jews were on the average wealthier, more educated, more urban, and in many ways better off than the average French citizen. Jews had similarly risen to considerable prominence in the arts and sciences. One observer commented that in the French *lycées* (the elite high schools)

> the Jewish boys topped the list. They understood all the problems, handed in the best compositions, and collected most of the prizes at the end of the year. There was no vying with them; they were far ahead of us. ... Math, languages, literature, everything seemed to be their forte. [183 *p. 406*]

The Great Depression hit France with less force than Germany, resentments over the rise of the Jews in France were less notable in the late 1870s and early 1880s, and anti-Jewish political initiatives were unimportant. That is not to say that rumblings of discontent were completely absent. French theorists of race, such as Gobineau, and of anti-Semitism, such as Proudhon, had been prominent since the early part of the century; already by the 1840s many works had appeared describing the Jews as 'rulers' or 'kings' of the new capitalistic era, with the Rothschilds as favored targets. With the victory of the republic in 1871–75, the Catholic right was increasingly fearful that the republicans – who were, as far as many Catholics were concerned, mostly atheists, Protestants, and Jews – would try to 'dechristianize' the country.

Financial scandals involving Jews were no less notorious than in Germany. One of particular importance had to do with the ill-fated efforts by the French to build a canal through Panama (1881–89). The intermediaries between the Panama Company and the French Chamber of Deputies were almost exclusively Jews, and they were exposed as bribing parliamentary delegates – over a hundred delegates and ministers of state were implicated – to cover up mismanagement of the project. Facing exposure, the Jewish intermediaries blackmailed one another, and one of them finally confessed, releasing information to the anti-Semitic press before committing suicide.

The collapse of the Panama project was not only a humiliation for France but meant that thousands of French small investors lost their savings. The anti-Semitic potential of the whole sorry episode was ably tapped by Edouard Drumont, whose two-volume book, *Jewish France* (1886), had sold over 100,000 copies in a single year. Drumont was a journalist of middling talent and dubious integrity, but he persuaded many that he was a fearless crusader against government corruption and Jewish subversion. His book was a compendium of everything negative about the Jews that he could find, or dream up. Most of the familiar themes were there: Jewish machinations to control the state, economy, and press; Jewish racial arrogance; Jewish financial trickery, with the peculiarly French charge that there was a clandestine Jewish *Syndicat*, a kind of Jewish Mafia, behind it all.

These developments of the late 1880s and early 1890s helped set the stage for the Dreyfus Affair. After Dreyfus had been arrested in the autumn of 1894, Drumont's newspaper announced, with brazen falsity, that the disgraced captain had confessed to everything. Since the Panama scandal had ended a short time before in a trial that was widely considered a whitewash, with Jewish bribery determining the outcome, Drumont warned that Dreyfus's rich relatives would contrive to get him released. When Dreyfus was actually found guilty by a military court and sentenced to life imprisonment on Devil's Island, it was the cause for widespread rejoicing.

But the passions awakened by the trial itself were relatively minor compared to what was to come two years later, as evidence began to surface that Dreyfus had been wrongly convicted. Demands for a new trial developed into 'the Affair,' causing much of France's politically active population to line up passionately on one side or another. The Anti-Dreyfusards denounced the new evidence as just another Jewish trick, produced by Jewish bribery; the Dreyfusards found the evidence persuasive and demanded that truth and justice be served, whatever the price. The price, in the eyes of many on the political right, was to defame and undermine the army, thereby jeopardizing French national security, at a time of great military vulnerability to Germany.

The role of anti-Semitism in Dreyfus's arrest and conviction was less decisive than widely believed at the time and for many years afterward [107 *p. 94 ff.*]. The evidence against him was at first persuasive to many who were not anti-Semitic. But the vehemence of the hatred expressed for Jews as the Dreyfus Affair heated up suggested to many observers at the time and subsequently that powerful and deeply irrational resentments against Jews were just under the surface, requiring only a proper catalyst to cause them to burst forth. The Jewish question was not about to be solved so smoothly as many had assumed. Indeed, after the outbursts during the Affair, that question seemed far more intractable than previously believed.

Such conclusions must be taken seriously and have been widely influential, but against them must also be placed some important considerations. The Anti-Dreyfusards were the final losers in the Affair;

Dreyfus's innocence was finally demonstrated beyond a reasonable doubt, and the Dreyfusards turned their victory in the Affair to political advantage, pushing forward a secular, militantly anti-Catholic agenda in the chamber of deputies. On the other hand, those left-wing political victories certainly did not eliminate anti-Semitism among large numbers of Frenchmen on the right. The victory of the Dreyfusards seemed only to intensify the anti-Jewish hatred many felt, leading them to conclude that the Jews had won again, with their trickery and behind-the-scenes power – but a day of reckoning would come.

Many German Jews followed the Affair with mixed emotions. Most had been admirers of French democracy, nourishing hopes that Germany would develop in political directions similar to those in France after 1871. The Affair caused many of them to ask if they were finally not better off in their own country, where law and order were more secure, and where political anti-Semitism, after its early showing, failed to gain a significant following.

However, negative feelings about Jews in Germany did not necessarily decline in the same way that political anti-Semitism did, particularly in a country like Germany where a large part of the intellectual elite tended to disdain politics. A number of scholars have argued that Jew-hatred of a more intellectual, or 'spiritual' sort deepened in these years, one that was all the more 'Germanic' for its lack of a clear political expression. There is little question that a more tribalistic nationalism was developing in some quarters in Germany, even while the internationalist social-democratic left was growing steadily. Indeed, German nationalism evolved into more paranoiac directions partly in reaction to that growth, which by the elections of 1912 had reached around one-third of the vote. Many concluded that it would only be a matter of a few years before the Social Democrats would gain an absolute majority in the Reichstag – a nightmare for conservatives and German nationalists.

The assertion that an anti-Semitic 'Germanic ideology' was embedding itself ever deeper in the psyches of Germany's intellectual classes has much engaging evidence to support it. The Belle Epoque throughout Europe witnessed renewed interest in irrationalist, anti-liberal ideas, prominently those of Friedrich Nietzsche. Although his writings were characterized by a subtlety and ambiguity that were worlds away from the mindless crudities of later Nazis, many Nazis claimed him as an inspiration, and that claim made some sense in terms of Nietzsche's calls for a return to the aristocratic, warrior virtues of the ancient Greeks, abandoning the 'slave morality' of

Christianity. That he was in fact no anti-Semite was either ignored or unappreciated by Nazis later claiming to speak in his name.

Among the more influential 'Germanic Idealists' was Julius Langbehn, whose work has been described by one scholar as spreading a 'mixture of cultural despair and nationalist hope' among Germany's reading public and artistic elite. Modernism was Langbehn's target, and 'science' the source of all, as far as he was concerned, that was hateful and destructive in the modern world. Anti-modernism was already a familiar theme of anti-Semitism, and Langbehn took up the theme with a peculiar Germanic passion and obscurity. The highly urbanized, educated, and politically liberal Jews of imperial Germany and Austria were an all too attractive symbol for him of a destructive modern capitalism and urbanity. Still, even Langbehn does not fit comfortably into a proto-Nazi mold. For all his attacks on modern liberal Jews, he did not in fact revile Jews as an essentially unchangeable race, and he interestingly regarded Orthodox Jews to be a potentially valuable component of the German people. He expressed a deep admiration for a number of Jews in history.

The writings of other influential anti-Semitic Germanic ideologists of the Belle Epoque, later claimed by the Nazis, were similarly marked by significantly non-Nazi principles. One of the most virulent was Paul de Lagarde, whose antimodernist rage exceeded even that of Langbehn. He described Jewish capitalists as 'trichnae and bacilli' who should be 'exterminated as quickly and thoroughly as possible' [170 *p. 93*]. Yet at the same time he had no use for race theory, which he regarded as a crude form of scientific materialism. And such materialism was for him as for Langbehn a main source of the evils of modern times. True Germanism, he intoned, was a matter of the spirit, not of blood or race. What he hated about modern Jews was not their race but their ideas. Modern Jews 'destroy all faith and spread materialism. ... They are the carriers of decay and pollute every national culture' [170 *p. 92*]. Given such words, it may come as a surprise to learn that Lagarde, like Langbehn, had close Jewish friends – who of course had freed themselves from 'Jewish' ideas.

No doubt the best known and most influential of the Germanic ideologists was Houston Stewart Chamberlain. His anti-Semitic racism is pervasive, and his connections to Nazism unusually clear, in part because he lived into the postwar years and appeared to give his blessings to Hitler personally before his death in 1927. Yet there was much about Chamberlain, too, that fits awkwardly into a proto-Nazi mold. His book, a literary sensation in 1900 and best-seller for many years afterward, *The Foundations of the Twentieth Century*, makes a revealing comparison to Marr's plebeian best-seller of 1879, in that Chamberlain's lengthy tome was enthusiastically acclaimed by some of the world's most prestigious figures, among them George Bernard Shaw, Albert Schweitzer, and Winston Churchill. The distinguished American historian Carl Becker wrote in a review of the book that 'one despairs of conveying an adequate idea' of its 'brilliant originality,' 'keen analysis,' and 'trenchant humor' [49 *pp. 463–6*].

Chamberlain may be considered an heir to and most influential spokesman for the belief in racial determinism to be seen in such earlier thinkers as Disraeli, Renan, Gobineau, Dühring, and Marr. Chamberlain was particularly concerned with the implications of race mixing. And he saw a mostly baleful influence of the Semites in history because of Semitic intolerance, vengefulness, and duplicity. Yet, as was true of many other self-styled 'scientific' thinkers, Renan most notably, his definition of race was anything but clear and consistent. He wrote that 'the term Jew ... denotes a special way of thinking and feeling;' if a 'purely humanized' Jew abandons 'the law of Moses' and 'contempt for others' he is 'no longer a Jew because, by renouncing the ideas of Judaism, he ipso facto has left that nationality' [31 *p. 30*]. In short, this man, who became a Nazi icon, denied what would be a fundamental Nazi belief, that Jewish race and character were both intertwined and immutable. Moreover, in a way that would be unthinkable for Hitler or other leading Nazis, Chamberlain claimed that he had 'remarkably many Jews or half-Jews as friends,' to whom he remained 'remarkably close.' His book was dedicated to a retired Jewish professor under whom he had once studied.

KARL LUEGER AND 'INSINCERE' ANTI-SEMITISM

Outside the German Reich, in the aforementioned 'German cultural sphere,' anti-Semitism registered clearer victories in the political arena. Such was the case most famously in Vienna, where the anti-Semitic mayor Karl Lueger held office from 1897 to 1910. These were years that overlapped with Hitler's own residence in that city. Indeed, Hitler would later make admiring references to Lueger in *Mein Kampf*, and it is usually assumed that Hitler modeled his own political activity on Lueger's.

Lueger may be seen not only as the most successful anti-Semitic politician before 1914 but a 'modern' one, with a pronounced Viennese flavor. His style and methods had much in common with big-city politicians elsewhere, in both Europe and the United States. He was devious, demagogic, opportunistic, and corrupt. At the same time he got things done, perfecting what has been called 'municipal socialism,' making life in the city more attractive and healthy for its common citizens, and winning a dazzling popularity in the process. Lueger was able to patch together previously separate or even hostile political constituencies and programs, notably populist indignation against banks and financiers, on the one hand, and the philosophy of the Christian Socials, on the other, that spoke out against the destructive impact of modern city life.

In a metropolis like Vienna, where Jewish numbers had increased about thirty times since the early part of the century, and where the Rothschilds were a large, much-discussed presence, attacks on Jews were an irresistible political temptation. Lueger built on anti-Semitic political bases dating from at least the 1880s, when the fiercely racist and Pan-German politician, Georg von Schönerer, had attracted much attention but relatively few votes. While similarly exploiting anti-Jewish resentments, Lueger was able to project a more genial image than von Schönerer had. Lueger was a master of public relations; he attended weddings, funerals, and baptisms by the hundreds. While himself well educated, he often spoke in the slangy dialect of the city, effectively projecting an image of a tough defender of the little man against the haughty, selfish upper classes and big-money interests.

Even in Lueger's case, however, one has to question how much it was doctrinaire racial anti-Semitism that motivated him, or indeed how much damage he actually did to Jews and Jewish interests while he was mayor. When reproached for his many Jewish contacts and compromises with Jewish interests, he allegedly quipped 'I decide who is a Jew!' His political cynicism or 'insincere anti-Semitism' was further revealed in comments he made in a special meeting with the leaders of Viennese Jewry:

> I dislike the Hungarian Jews even more than the Hungarians, but I am not really an enemy of our Viennese Jews. They are not so bad and we cannot do without them. My Viennese always want to have a good rest. The Jews are the only ones who always want to be active. [138 *p. 204*]

And in spite of his sometimes ugly attacks on Jews, the measures he actually took against them did most of them little material harm. There was no Jewish exodus from the city when he became mayor. Quite the contrary, Jews continued to move into Vienna in numbers comparable to earlier years. And what has been called 'the Golden Age of Viennese Jewry' overlapped almost exactly with the period in which Lueger was mayor.

NAZISM IN THE MAKING?

In attempting to arrive at a balanced account of the origins and development of modern racial-political anti-Semitism, one must of course guard against unduly minimizing the relevance of this period in preparing Europe for Nazism and the Holocaust. The widespread belief today that in these years a reservoir of hatred for Jews was somehow being filled for future use undoubtedly has some merit. That the Nazis crudely misunderstood or misused the thought of men like Nietzsche is true; that elements of Nietzsche's thought lent themselves to such a misuse is also true. One must doubt if Hitler carefully read Nietzsche, Chamberlain, or even Marr. He had little interest in the varieties or subtleties of the thought of the anti-Semites before 1914 – and even less in why they had so many Jewish friends – and his lack of interest was shared by most Nazis.

Certainly the Holocaust is not understandable without examining the thinkers and political activists of the 1870s to 1914. On the other hand, let us hope that our own standards of historical understanding will be more discriminating than those of the Nazis, for there *were* important differences between most of these men and most Nazis. Few anti-Semites of the pre-1914 period demonized the Jews in the same way, and few spoke with such crudity. And even when we encounter language among some of them that seems to suggest violence, it is doubtful that most of those conjuring up murderous images actually had in mind what the Nazis finally did.

Anti-Semites of this period typically used a language closer to the angry exaggerations seen in 'normal' political rhetoric. Treitschke said unkind and unfair things, but they were difficult to distinguish in quality from the unkind and unfair things said in most political clashes in most countries, including the United States and Great Britain, in these years. Lueger was cynical and corrupt, but such qualities were amply displayed by other politicians of the day, even in liberal democracies. A generalization to be found in many works on anti-Semitism is that Jew-hatred has something mysteriously intoxicating about it, and there is some truth to that. Yet what is also impressive about anti-Semitic writings of the pre-1914 period is how little in fact they intoxicated their readers toward fanatical hatred of Jews. If a book like Chamberlain's *Foundations* is judged to have such influence, how can we explain that so many people read it, praised it to the skies, and then later became unshakably anti-Nazi – including the most famous anti-Nazi of all, Winston Churchill? And if men as diverse as Renan and Marr imbibed heavily of the mysteriously intoxicating potion of Jew-hatred, how was it that they 'sobered up' and renounced their earlier anti-Jewish pronouncements? If indeed comparable to a drug or a cancer (the other common simile), anti-Semitism found many who could take it and leave it, or acquire some of it and not be consumed by it.

The tendency to describe Nazism as some sort of essence building from a remote period in German or European history and growing steadily, inexorably, on its own inner resources – again, as a cancer – until finding ultimate expression between 1933 and 1945 is finally a mystical and discredited form of historical understanding. What has also been termed 'the gathering storm' or 'rising tide' interpretation of Nazism must confront what by now is a massive amount of contrary evidence. It was anything but obvious from the evidence at hand before 1914 that anti-Semitism was growing steadily stronger, especially in Germany, or that Europe was moving toward a mass murder of its Jewish population. Much had happened that made it difficult to retain the optimism of mid-century, when progress and reason seemed all-conquering, but even the most disheartening of events, such as the Dreyfus Affair, were not without a brighter side: the struggle against bigotry, in short, while more of a challenge than previously believed, was still not without hope. French Jews did not emigrate, did not embrace Zionism, or in other ways abandon the new identity that their forefathers had assumed at the time of the French Revolution. And if any pollster had asked Europeans at the turn of the century where large-scale violence against Jews might most likely occur, surely the consensus would have been Russia or Romania. After the Dreyfus Affair, France might have been named, or Austria, given Lueger's successes, but almost certainly not Germany.

Of course, few would have understood by 'large-scale' a figure so monstrous as six million; the numbers that might have occurred to them would have been hundreds, perhaps thousands. In short, the ghastly dimensions of future tragedies were unimaginable – for Jews and for the rest of Europe's population. In an article for the 1911 edition of the *Encyclopedia Britannica* the Jewish activist Lucien Wolf wrote that the anti-Semitic movement throughout Europe had exhausted itself, leaving no permanent mark of a productive nature. His further comments about that movement are revealing in a number of regards (including his concept of race):

Its [the anti-Semitic movement's] extravagant accusations ... have resulted in the vindication of the Jewish character. Its agitation ... has helped to transfer Jewish solidarity from a religious to a racial basis. The bond of a common race ... has given a new spirit and a new source of strength to Judaism when ... the revolts against dogma were sapping its essentially religious foundations. In the whole history of Judaism, perhaps, there have been no more numerous and remarkable instances of reversion to the faith than in the period in question. [187 *pp. 459–60*]

Wolf could no more imagine the future than anyone else. Within three years Europe would tumble into an orgy of self-destruction and bloodshed with few parallels in history. After 1914, the rise of the Jews became an ever greater issue, with greater paradoxes and tragic consequences. The charge that the Jews were plotting to take over the world would gain much wider credence once the Bolsheviks, widely if inaccurately believed to be mostly Jews, took over Russia. And Jews would rise to prominence in a number of other countries, including Germany, where they had previously been prevented from doing so. In short, the events beginning in 1914 would change everything.

4 WAR, REVOLUTION, FASCISM, 1914–33

It would be difficult to overemphasize the importance of World War I for the origins of Nazism and the Holocaust. The titanic clash of Europe's major powers and the seemingly endless slaughter at the front resulted in a staggering toll of death and destruction, giving rise by 1917 to mutinies and revolution. The intervention of the Americans in the same year allowed a final victory for the Entente powers, France and Britain, a victory that contributed to a collapse of those empires (Austro-Hungarian, German, and Turkish) that had been allied against the Entente. But the year 1917 witnessed an even more portentous collapse of the Russian Empire, until then allied with France and Britain. Many believed the rise of the Bolsheviks to power in Russia would be short-lived; Lenin and his followers were believed to be wild-eyed fanatics who, even if capable of exploiting the chaos of the summer and fall of 1917, could never retain power. But they did, with finally vast implications.

The tragedies of 1914–19 gave rise to further calamities in the interwar period – run-away inflation, economic depression, the rise of the Nazis, mass murder in the Soviet Union. We might add to the phrase 'no Hitler no Holocaust' the equally apt 'no World War I no Holocaust,' since Hitler's own experiences as a front-line soldier had much to do with his later successes and program. Similarly, the Bolshevik Revolution provided him with one of his most effective propaganda tools, the threat of 'Jewish' Communism.

In early August 1914, Jews in most countries joined the general enthusiasm for war and hoped that their demonstrated willingness to risk their lives at the front would silence the long-standing allegations of Jewish disloyalty and cowardice. German Jews joined in the exhilarating anticipation of rapid victory that united Germans of all stations. Germany's mission in modern times, the triumph of German idealism, was about to be confirmed yet again on the battlefield. One

Jewish observer wrote that for German Jews the outbreak of war was an 'unbelievable experience, an intoxicating happiness which enabled them to forget their complicated egos and be able to participate in the fate of the fatherland with millions of others' [140 *pp. 222–3*]. Even the Social Democrats, after initial efforts to preserve the peace, finally joined in the general frenzy for war and rapid victory.

H. S. Chamberlain wrote that after August 1914 Jews in Germany were no longer visible as Jews, 'for they are doing their duty as Germans' [127 *p. 411*]. A number of German Jews won praise and favorable visibility from the authorities, perhaps most notably Ernst Lissauer, whose 'Hate Song Against England' became wildly popular in Germany and earned him a decoration from Kaiser Wilhelm II [127 *p. 30*]. The German government clamped down on the anti-Semitic press and warned anti-Semitic activists to cease their divisive attacks.

Even in Russia, where relations between the government and the Jews by 1914 were incomparably more poisoned than was the case with any other major power, emotional scenes of Jewish–Gentile reconciliation in the name of the national cause were reported in the opening days of the war. Prominent Jewish leaders gave rousing speeches about how hundreds of thousands of Jews across the Russian Empire were marching enthusiastically to the front in the name of Mother Russia. But such scenes were more short-lived in Russia than in any other country, in part because Russia met humiliating defeat in the opening battles. One historian of the period wrote that, behind the public rhetoric, most Russian Jews did not support the oppressive tsarist regime. He quoted a Jewish memoirist as writing that Jews 'eagerly awaited the defeat of Russia in war. ... Germany and Austria ... are not considered our enemies' [130 *p. 24*].

Much of the fighting on the eastern front occurred in the Pale of Settlement, with inevitably dire consequences for all the people in the area, especially Jews, because Russia's military leaders believed the Jews likely to collaborate with the German and Austro-Hungarian armies. As the German forces advanced rapidly into the Pale in late 1914, the retreating Russian armies drove some half million Jews back into Russian territory. As the war lumbered on, the death toll in the area mounted appallingly, from disease, exposure, and malnutrition as much as from direct military causes. The total by the end of the war was something like 4.5 million, Jews and non-Jews.

German military leaders sought to exploit the anti-Russian sentiments of the population by acts of kindness to Jews and other subject peoples. Much Jewish testimony praises the humane treatment of Jews by the German occupying forces. One woman later wrote that the Germans 'treated the Jews marvelously. ... They gave each child sweets and biscuits. These were different Germans, a different period' [82 *pp. 423–5*]. The general in charge, Erich Ludendorff, took many steps during the German occupation to win over the Jewish population, repealing tsarist anti-Jewish legislation, dedicating synagogues, and attending the Yiddish-language theater with his officers.

THE JEW AS SHIRKER AND WAR PROFITEER

As the seemingly endless battles of 1916 on the western front took hundreds of thousands of lives without breaking the military stalemate, war-weariness also began to spread there. Since Germany and Austria-Hungary ultimately experienced defeat, anti-Semitism had especially great potential in those lands, but before that defeat the enthusiastic unity of August 1914 had begun to dissolve. In October 1916, the German minister of war announced that an inquiry was being initiated, later known as the 'Jew Count,' to determine if Jews were somehow avoiding front-line service. He defended this initiative as necessary to counter the proliferating rumors that Jews, using money and connections, were escaping the most dangerous duties at the front. However, the results of the Jew Count were not published during the war, leading many to conclude that the allegations had been confirmed by the inquiry but were considered too inflammatory to release. (The statistics gathered are not easily summarized, but they showed, among other things, that German Jews were awarded some 30,000 Iron Crosses for gallantry at the front and died there in roughly comparable numbers to Catholics or Protestants [6; 108 *p. 399*].)

The following excerpt from a much-noted article entitled 'Hear O Israel,' written shortly before World War I by a prominent German businessman, suggests the extent to which beliefs concerning the lack of military virtues among Jews were still alive in German-speaking lands:

> Your east Mediterranean appearance is not very well appreciated by the northern tribes. You should therefore be more careful ... [not to become] the laughing stock of a race brought up in a strictly military fashion. As soon as you have recognized your unathletic build, your narrow shoulders, your clumsy feet, your sloppy, roundish shape, you will resolve to dedicate a few generations to the renewal of your outer appearance. [122 *p. 232*]

The author of these lines, Walther Rathenau, was a prominent German Jew. He was also an ardent German nationalist who played a major role in organizing Germany's war effort. After the war, he would become Germany's first Jewish foreign minister.

That a prominent Jew could pen such lines suggests some of the peculiarities of the German situation. That he became foreign minister and then was assassinated in 1922 by right-wing fanatics offers yet more evidence of the bewildering contradictions of German politics. Why would such a man be hated by the German radical Right? A common answer has been that utter irrationality determined that hatred, driven by an unyielding anti-Semitic fantasy that a Jew, no matter what his public face, would always be a traitor. In Rathenau's case, his great wealth and many financial connections made him especially suspect. He was notorious for the observation, in another article, that a self-selected circle of some 300 men guided the destiny of Europe. He became, like the Rothschilds, a symbol of a new, ever more extensive power that Jews allegedly wielded behind the scenes.

Rathenau's role during the war also made him many enemies. As director of the Raw Materials Section of the army, he exercised extensive control over strategic raw materials, favoring larger concerns because of their greater efficiency. Among the favored firms were a disproportionate number led by Jews, many of whom made enormous profits during the war – as did of course many non-Jewish firms. Had Germany won the war, those war-time profits might not have so rankled, but Germans whose lives were ruined by the conflict, whether soldiers of the front or small and uncompetitive businessmen, often harbored a fierce hatred of those who had grown rich during it.

Charges of Jewish profiteering were even more widespread in other areas of Europe. In Budapest, the business classes during the war were reported to be 'singularly gross in profiteering.' They were also widely recognized to be around 90 percent Jewish. The noted historian and Jew Oszkar Jaszi was appalled at the contrast between the luxury of the Budapest business world, overwhelmingly Jewish, and the misery of the war front. He sensed storm-clouds of retribution on the horizon [120 *p. 105*].

The image of the Jew as avoiding front-line service gained credence even in Britain, where Dreyfus had won wide sympathy and where prewar anti-Semitism had been notably weaker than on the Continent. British hostility in these regards was directed at Jewish immigrants from Russia, many of whom showed a distinct aversion to fighting on the same side as the tsar's armies. A police report in

1917, seeking to explain why anti-Jewish rioting had broken out in Leeds and London's East End, wrote that there were

> large numbers of alien Russian Jews of military age ... who can be constantly seen promenading about our principal streets and the various pleasure resorts. ... Members of the Christian population have been heard to ask why these men are not serving in the Army as the husbands, brothers, and sons of the Christian population. [76 p. 131]

By war's end, a large part of Europe's population accepted the image of Jews as using their wiles, high-level contacts, or financial leverage to avoid front-line service and profit from the war. Such an image was all the more plausible because by late 1916 men of all backgrounds were doing what they could to evade orders to move to the front. The senseless suffering of the war was ever more resented, the inflated patriotic rhetoric of the opening months ever more generally mocked.

It is revealing that after the Bolsheviks assumed power, the belief that Jews avoided the front continued to play a role even in this revolutionary government, known for its denunciations of tsarist anti-Semitism. A little more than a year after the Bolshevik takeover, Leon Trotsky, at the head of the Red Army and himself Jewish, was outraged by the many reports that Jews in the new revolutionary army had taken up office jobs in highly disproportionate numbers. He angrily assigned many of them to dangerous combat zones [41 p. 70].

A point that needs to be taken into consideration in these charges of Jewish shirking is the substantially different social structure of the Jews, especially in Russia, where Jewish literacy was distinctly higher than that of non-Jews. That Jews would get a disproportionate number of office jobs or other jobs of executive authority requiring literacy is not surprising, especially in a revolutionary regime that took over from a reactionary one that had excluded Jews. But for those peasant or working-class recruits sent to the front the rationality of this situation might not have been so apparent or persuasive.

THE JEW AS SUBVERSIVE

A related image spread rapidly after late 1917: the Jew as fanatical revolutionary destroyer. This image blended with older images of the Jew as mocker and exploiter of Christians and enemy of Christian society. Now it was believed that Jews had seized control of the largest country in the world. In typically paradoxical ways, then, Jews were seen as 'destroying,' both as capitalists and as agitators among the angry, radicalized masses.

The belief that the Bolsheviks were overwhelmingly Jewish spread widely after the Bolshevik revolution. And that belief was embraced not only by sworn enemies of the Jews or by people on the fringes of respectability. Winston Churchill, who had earlier won strong support from Jewish voters in Britain, intoned that

> This mysterious race has been chosen for the supreme manifestation, both of the divine and the diabolical. ... [Jews have been] the mainspring of every subversive movement during the nineteenth century. ... [They have now] gripped the Russian people by the hair of their heads and have become practically the undisputed masters of that enormous empire. [89 *p. 100*]

Walther von Kaiserlingk, the German admiralty's chief of operations, visited Russia in the winter of 1917–18 and described the new Bolshevik regime as run by Jews in the interests of Jews, 'insanity in power.' The German Kaiser soon declared that the Russian people had been 'turned over to the vengeance of the Jews, who are connected to all the Jews of the world' [136 *pp. 585–6*].

The issue of how many Jews were in the Bolshevik Party, and later in the international Communist movement, has been much debated, although there is little question that most Bolsheviks were not Jewish. Still, simple statistics can obscure important truths; the issue of the role of Jews in the Bolshevik Party (or Communist Party, as it was called after 1919) presents a particularly revealing example of the interplay of fantasy and reality in anti-Semitism. Much depends on the definition of 'Jew.' If a very strict definition is followed (someone born a Jew and living by traditional Jewish law), no Jews were to be found among the Bolsheviks. On the other hand, quite a few Bolsheviks, especially at the upper echelons of the party, had Jewish ancestry or were married to Jews, certainly more than the roughly 10 percent of the Russian Empire's western territories that was Jewish. The main point was that for most Russian nationalists the very idea of having *any* Jews, however defined, in positions of power in Mother Russia was wholly unacceptable, a nightmare.

The case of V. I. Lenin is instructive. Most Russian counter-revolutionaries had no doubt of Lenin's Jewish identity. Given his revolutionary ideas and the large number of Jews in his entourage, he simply 'had to be Jewish' and could not be a 'real' Russian. In truth his father, a school principal, was a member of the tsarist service nobility whose ethnic identity was Great Russian. Yet his ancestry was a remarkable mix, not uncommon among those who assumed Great Russian ethnicity in the nineteenth century: on his father's side, Kalmyk (an Asiatic ethnic group) and Swedish; on his mother's, German and Jewish. So Lenin did have a Jewish grandfather, although that grandfather had converted to Christianity and his descendents did not consider themselves to be Jewish.

Russian anti-Semites spoke of 'jewified' non-Jews and of those who remained 'foreign' although born in Russia. Lenin fitted into that category, not only because of his single Jewish grandparent (Jewish enough to have fallen under suspicion in Nazi Germany, or been accepted as a citizen by the state of Israel) but also because of his many Jewish fellow revolutionaries and his long residence outside of Russia. He remarked once to the novelist Maxim Gorky that 'an intelligent Russian is almost always a Jew or someone with Jewish blood in his veins.' He similarly believed that 'the Jews furnished a particularly high percentage ... of leaders of the revolutionary movement' [79 *p. 134*]. Similar remarks were commonplace in Russia and elsewhere. The French socialist leader and Jew, Leon Blum, wrote that 'the collective impulse' of the Jews 'leads them toward revolution; their critical powers ... drive them to destroy every idea, every traditional form that does not agree with the facts or cannot be justified by reason.' Revolutionary socialism, he asserted, was a modern expression of 'the ancient spirit of the Jewish race' [184 *p. 83*].

Trotsky, who easily qualifies as the second most important Bolshevik after Lenin at the time of the revolution and whose parents were both Jewish, had arrived at a rather different evaluation of Jews. He thought they were on the whole of little worth to the revolutionary movement because they so tenaciously resisted joining the manual working class, retaining a 'petty-bourgeois consciousness.' Like Marx, Trotsky thought of Jews as having been so long associated with handling money that their characters were hopelessly stained by it. Trotsky's biographer, Isaac Deutscher, has referred to him as 'the prophet armed,' a man who epitomized the revolutionary message of ancient Israel in modern guise [40].

A revealing example of a 'jewified' non-Jew was the head of the Secret Police, or Cheka, Felix Dzerzhinsky. In origin a member of the Polish gentry, he worked as a young man with Jewish revolutionary movements, learned Yiddish, and had a number of romances with

Jewish women, finally marrying one. Another was Mikhail Kalinin, of Russian peasant background, who became the president of the new Soviet state. A man of limited education, he had an admiration for Jews so heart-felt that he was labeled 'more Jewish than the Jews.' In a much-noted speech describing a pogrom, he broke down crying and was so overcome by grief that he was unable to finish [130 *p. 213*].

Many of the other non-Jews in high positions in the new Communist state were in various ways also 'outsiders,' often belonging to non-Russian minority groups or descendents of oppressed religious minorities. Josef Stalin, who would later rise to rule the Soviet Union, was Georgian. Known for his crudeness and his relatively limited education, Stalin was suspicious and envious of the many Jewish intellectuals in the party. In later life, he revealed growing anti-Semitic tendencies, although never in an openly doctrinal way. He worked closely with Jews in the early history of the party and retained a few advisers who were Jewish through the 1930s and 1940s. But he saw to it that most other Jewish leaders of the party were eliminated in the purges of the mid-1930s.

Other examples could be cited to illustrate just how elusive the question of Jews in the Communist movement is, but one point should emerge with reasonable clarity: the 'Jews' that many believed were ruling Russia were often 'jewified' non-Jews. And even when having Jewish parents, revolutionary Jews were unlike the great majority of Jews in Russia; Communist revolutionaries by definition had broken with Judaism, and most had also distanced themselves from Jewish secular culture. They usually spoke Russian, not Yiddish, and many had been born outside of the Pale, growing up with extensive non-Jewish contacts. For such reasons, the exact percentage of Jews in the Bolshevik Party is impossible to state. Any figure that one might come up with would be burdened with major qualifications, but there is little question that Jews were heavily overrepresented in the upper echelons of the Communist movement in Russia and elsewhere.

In considering, then, whether it was a mere prejudice, a baseless fantasy, to believe that Bolshevism and Jewishness had some sort of peculiar connection, one needs to remember that both the non-Jewish enemy of the Communists, Churchill, and the non-Jewish leader of the Communist movement itself, Lenin, firmly believed that there was such a connection, as did most Jewish revolutionaries themselves. In short, if the notion of 'Jewish Communism' was an anti-Semitic fantasy unconnected to any reality, a large percentage of the world in 1917 embraced that fantasy, and it would be many years before a more strictly accurate perception began to emerge.

VISIONS OF JEWISH POWER

Even more fantastic visions of Jewish power were spreading in these years. One of the seemingly most outlandish was that Jewish capitalists and revolutionaries had joined forces in their quest to conquer the world. The assassins of Rathenau believed he was a member of that vast conspiracy. Indeed, since the early part of the century, Nicholas II had considered himself at 'war' not only with his own Jewish subjects but their Jewish supporters and contacts throughout the world. Such beliefs were much intensified after Russia's humiliating defeat in the Russo-Japanese War (1904–5), followed by revolution in 1905. Nicholas could not believe that his own Russian people were behind such a challenge to his divinely sanctioned autocratic authority; it had to be 'foreigners,' in particular the Jews. That men like Trotsky rose to leadership of the 1905 revolution only served to confirm such beliefs. In some ways even more alarming to Nicholas and his advisers was the role that the American financier Jacob Schiff played to prevent Russia from getting much-needed financial support for the war against the Japanese, while simultaneously providing financial support to the Japanese. Schiff and other Jewish activists had long worked to put pressure on the tsarist regime to abandon its anti-Jewish policies, but by this time he thought more in terms of bringing down the tsar. For such reasons, he also fed money into various revolutionary movements inside Russia [108 *pp. 302–3*].

Schiff boasted that Russia would have to face the fact that 'international Jewry is a power after all.' Simon Wolf, another Jewish activist and confidant of American presidents, remarked that 'in the United States the Jews form an important factor in the formation of public opinion and in the control of finances. ... [t]hey are exercising an all-potent ... influence' [20 *pp. 108–9*]. This boasting, while transparently designed to impress the Russians, nonetheless constituted solid proof for many others that powerful Jews of all nations and political persuasions were indeed working together. A prominent English journalist concluded that the Jews were making 'monotonous progress toward the mastery of the world' [163 *pp. 148–9*].

Given how widespread such beliefs were, it is not surprising that one of the most notorious forgeries of modern times, the *Protocols of the Elders of Zion*, was given credence by some well educated and otherwise well informed observers. Patched together by the Russian secret police before World War I, the *Protocols* supposedly were an account of secret meetings of international Jewry's leaders, describing how Jews exploited various modern trends to undermine the societies in which they lived: liberalism, Marxism, capitalism, and gutter journalism were all cleverly manipulated by Jews. First persuasively exposed as a forgery by *The Times* in London in 1921, the *Protocols* nonetheless continued to be widely accepted as authentic. Henry Ford reprinted them in the 1920s, as did the Nazis, and most recently the Arab enemies of the state of Israel have propagated them.

The use of the *Protocols* by Arab anti-Zionists offers further insight into why they were given credence. Many asked how the Jews, supposedly a small, persecuted, and powerless minority, could accomplish such an astonishing goal – that is, to be given title to land inhabited by others and sacred to Christians as well as Moslems? The obvious answer for anti-Zionists and anti-Semites was 'only by demonic and clandestine power.' The Zionist movement itself, as it formed in the 1890s, seemed by any ordinary calculation the most hopeless of causes. That it sought to organize Jews all over the world to recover 'Zion' again spoke of powerful international organization; anti-Semites were convinced that there had to be much more to the movement than was visible from its public face. And once the Communist International had been set up in 1919, yet another plausible vehicle for the exercise of Jewish power was identified. And of course there were others, among them the Rothschilds, with their banking houses in most European capitals, and the French *Syndicat*, allegedly fronted by the Alliance Israélite Universelle, an organization that had been formed in France to aid oppressed or impoverished Jews throughout the world.

The belief in a conspiracy by Jews to dominate the world invites comparison with the Blood Libel, in that both seem to have taken on a life of their own, seemingly immune to repeated refutation by authoritative sources. Of course, there was much evidence of certain kinds of Jewish international collaboration, whereas nothing of the sort could be cited for the Blood Libel. At any rate, confirmation of the charge that Jews exercised vast international power was offered, so anti-Semites contended, once a Jewish homeland was established, first through the Balfour Declaration of the British government in late 1917 and then by measures taken under the League of Nations following the war; no powerless people could possibly have accomplished such things.

THE APPEARANCE OF FASCISM

Some observers believed Jews to be the 'winners' of the catastrophic events between 1914 and 1919. In the light of the tragedies experienced by Jews in those years, especially in the Pale of Settlement, such beliefs verge on the fantastic. Yet the charge of Jewish 'victory' had enough plausibility to persuade large numbers of people, especially those who thought of themselves as victims or losers in these years. Many whose anti-Jewish sentiments before 1914 had been relatively mild now cried out for violent measures. H. S. Chamberlain wrote, as Germany's fortunes in war worsened:

> The Jews are completely intoxicated by their success in Germany – first from the millions they have gained through the war, then because of the praise showered on them in all official quarters, and thirdly from the protection their machinations enjoy from the censor. Thus, they are beginning to lose their heads and to reach a degree of insolence which may allow us to hope for a flood-tide of reaction. May God grant it! [49 *p. 382*]

After Germany's defeat, General Ludendorff angrily wrote of how Germans had 'fought for their freedom, with weapons in hand, while Jews did business and betrayed' [127 *p. 37*]. German nationalists spoke of a 'stab in the back' by cowardly and treacherous politicians willing to sign a peace even when the armed forces remained 'undefeated in the field.' Those 'November Criminals' (the armistice was signed in November 1918) were mostly on the left, and of course the left was considered by conservatives to be dominated by the Jews. The panicked slogan 'the Jew is everywhere!' gained unprecedented credence.

Outraged nationalism and a profound fear of Communism were central to the fascist temper, but its traits were shifting and elusive, evolving in sometimes astonishing directions from 1919 to the outbreak of World War II. Fascists in all countries were more easily distinguished by what they were against than what they were for. In more general ways, fascism exploited a wide range of anxieties about the meaning of modern times, so intensified by developments from 1914 to 1919.

The association of Jews with modernism and the left, the broader belief that 'alien Jews' were plotting to take over the world, would make it seem that anti-Semitism was all too natural to fascism. And indeed most fascist movements made of the alien and subversive Jew a figure of central significance; 'the Jew' neatly combined in one potent symbol all that fascists were struggling against, from capitalist corruption to Communist fanaticism. But one of many striking paradoxes about fascism is that the original and model fascist movement in Italy was not anti-Semitic. On the contrary, Italian Jews were influential in the early fascist party and over-represented in its upper ranks, almost certainly more so than Jews were in the upper ranks of the Bolshevik Party.

The comparison is tricky, however, in that the Jewish population of the Russian Empire was proportionately around a hundred times larger than the Jewish population of Italy. Similarly different from the Russian scene, in modern Italy Jews were not oppressed; they had enjoyed full civil rights since the 1860s, and quite the opposite of being at war with the governing elites before 1914, they were to a significant degree integrated into the country's ruling castes.

Similarly, Benito Mussolini, the charismatic leader (*Duce*) of Italian fascism, had extensive and intimate Jewish contacts. Before the war, when he was active in the Italian socialist movement, he worked closely with a number of Jewish socialists and had romantic liaisons with several Jewish women, fathering a child by one. In his struggle to establish the fascist movement, Mussolini relied on the advice of his Jewish mistress from 1913 to the late 1920s, Margherita Sarfatti, 'the uncrowned queen of Italy.' She and her wealthy husband helped Mussolini to establish contacts with key elements of the Italian business elite, among whom were many Jews [28 *pp. 97–8*].

It would be a fool's errand to try to find consistency in a mind as opportunistic and fickle as Mussolini's, but in the 1920s and early 1930s he often spoke out strongly against racism. He also often expressed the belief that Jews were an important power in Europe, one that any statesman should avoid angering. He had little use for the Nazis before the mid-1930s and declared that 'Hitler's anti-Semitism has already brought him more enemies than is necessary' [124 *p. 31*]. He similarly expressed his opinion that 'anti-Semitism is foreign to the Italian people' [38 *p. 82*].

He was correct that anti-Jewish sentiments had played almost no role in modern Italian history. In the 1880s and 1890s, when anti-Semitic rumblings were to be heard in most other European countries, there was nothing in Italy of comparable dimensions. And indignation over Italy's 'mutilated victory' in World War I did not turn notably against its own Jewish population, which had rallied to the colors in World War I and died at the front in disproportionate numbers. One Italian Jew later recalled that her father, returning from the front, was 'deeply wounded' by the antiwar agitation of the left, which often entailed attacking soldiers who were wearing medals.

> He became convinced, like many other landowners of the time, that nothing could stop the 'Bolshevik hydra,' except a strong, new patriotic regime. ... More out of anger than ideology, he enrolled himself in the Fascist party, which was gaining strength and credibility with the help of enraged war veterans like himself. [158 *p. 40*]

Visiting Italy in 1927, Winston Churchill enthused: 'Duce, If I had been born Italian, I am sure that I should have been wholeheartedly with you from start to finish, in your triumphant struggle against the bestial appetites and passions of Leninism' [65 *p. 14*]. Tourists returned from Italy with praise for the new regime ('the trains run on time!'); the fascists had put an end to the constant strikes of the postwar period and instilled a much needed sense of discipline in the Italians.

The story of Mussolini's move toward an alliance with Nazi Germany, a move that by 1938 entailed the passage of anti-Semitic laws in Italy modeled on Germany's Nuremberg Laws of 1935, is well-known. What is often ignored is how little recognition Hitler gave, publicly or privately, to the role of Jews in the beginning years of Italy's fascist movement. And this lapse cannot be considered a trivial point: Hitler dogmatically asserted that Jews corrupted and undermined all that they touched. He also repeatedly emphasized that the Italian fascist movement was his model.

Hitler's silence about Jews in the Italian fascist movement coexisted with even more striking silences in his speeches and in *Mein Kampf* about his own friendly contacts with Jews before he began his political career in 1919. It would seem that if any European leader expressed a fanatical hatred of Jews after 1919, it was Hitler. Still, it is not difficult to understand how many observers could persuade themselves that his near hysterical ranting about Jews on one occasion but then 'statesman-like' pronouncements about them on another indicated that he was simply using anti-Semitism 'insincerely' as a political device to attract certain audiences. Jewish veterans' organizations in Germany were at first inclined to support Hitler's program, except for the extreme anti-Semitism. Other national-conservative Jewish groups expressed 'ambivalence' about Nazism rather than overt hostility to it [1 *p. 25*]. Similarly, for some Orthodox Jews, as indeed for many Zionists, Hitler's hostility merely confirmed what they had been arguing all along about the foolishness of those Jews who embraced a German national identity.

What we now appreciate is how different Hitler finally was from most earlier anti-Semites. Still, many of his contemporaries believed him capable of compromise and back-room deals. It was widely observed that he toned down his attacks on Jews in the late 1920s and early 1930s, transparently in hopes of seeming more respectable and thus widening his appeal. Revealingly, in 1928 Ludendorff angrily accused Hitler of abandoning the fight against the Jews, an accusation that Hitler did not much resist, commenting that in truth 'law-abiding Jews had little to fear' from his movement [1 *p. 26;* 124 *p. 49*]. His murkily defined 'anti-Semitism of reason' seemed to be asserting that the pogromist type of Jew-hatred characteristic of eastern Europe was not an acceptable policy for Germans. When the Nuremberg Laws were passed, declaring that Jews were no longer citizens but ostensibly recognizing their right as alien residents to make a living, Hitler let it be known that these measures represented the most moderate of the various drafts presented to him. He added that this was his 'last word on the Jewish question,' and that the laws finally established 'a basis on which the German people might be able to find a tolerable relationship with the Jewish people' [90 *pp. 235–6*].

It is plausible to consider Hitler's occasionally moderate pronouncements, continuing off and on through the mid-1930s, as merely tactical, cynically masking his murderous long-range plans. There is no question that Hitler was capable of ruthless deception, but there nonetheless do remain substantial uncertainties about the nature and evolution of his anti-Semitic program. A persuasive case can be made that his plans for the Jews evolved tentatively and gradually, from the rhetorical posturing and nebulous threats of a political neophyte, in the early 1920s, to the more precise but still poorly coordinated measures of the early 1940s. The peculiar dynamics of the totalitarian state he introduced meant that forces were unleashed, competing agencies within the Nazi movement, that pushed for developments that even he did not – could not – foresee. A few scholars (the 'Intentionalists') have asserted that the Holocaust was the straightforward enactment of ideas and plans already firmly set in Hitler's mind from the beginning of his political career, but most historians now accept a more complex scenario, involving an intricate interplay of hate-filled but inchoate intentions on Hitler's part, on the one hand, and concrete opportunities of an often unforeseeable nature, on the other.

What is particularly tantalizing is the evidence that Hitler had friendly rather than unfriendly relations with Jews before 1919 [175 *p. 29 ff.*]. After his mother's death, Hitler kept up a respectful correspondence with her Jewish doctor, including postcards signed 'your ever grateful Adolf Hitler' [117 *pp. 55, 358*]. Young Adolf had few friends in Vienna, but among them were a number of Jews, men for whom, again, he seems to have felt gratitude rather than resentment. While at the front in World War I, it was Hitler's Jewish commanding officer who recommended him for the Iron Cross [175 *pp. 61, 90*].

How did such a man become the raging anti-Semitic orator of the post-1919 period? In *Mein Kampf* Hitler refers to his 'inner soul struggles' while in Vienna; anti-Semitism at first seemed to him 'so monstrous, the accusations so boundless, that, tormented by the fear of doing injustice, I ... became anxious and uncertain' [74 *pp. 55–6*]. How could he reconcile what he read in the anti-Semitic press and experienced on the streets of Vienna with his esteem for the individual Jews he had known, or indeed the Jewish artists he so admired in Vienna's theaters?

Hitler wanted his readers to believe that he had arrived at his 'uncompromising' (a favorite word of his) anti-Semitism only after long reflection and serious reading. He presented his hatred, in short, as the product of a reasonable reaction to Jews as they 'really were' – which it took him quite some time to comprehend fully. This was of course similar to the argument made by modern anti-Semites since Marr: they were abandoning fantastic religious or superstitious visions and concentrating on a 'scientific' category, race, which determined Jewish character. Marr, too, avowed that he came to anti-Semitic conclusions only after long reflection and much close and finally disillusioning contact with Jews.

Most observers have of course not accepted Hitler's account; they have interpreted his hatred as based on sheer fantasy, on visions of The Jew grotesquely divorced from Jewish reality. Hitler had certainly encountered much evidence to support the conclusion that all Jews were *not* evil, yet he chose to pay decisive or public attention only to what he believed was evidence of their alien destructiveness. He ultimately embraced a vision of Jews that demonized them collectively, ignoring the great variety among Jews and insisting that they *all* poisoned everything they touched.

How and when this transformation occurred – indeed whether it was a genuine conversion – cannot be determined confidently, but much evidence points to the year 1919 itself, when Hitler, in despair over Germany's defeat, personally observed Communist revolutionaries in Bavaria, predominantly led by Jews [110 *p. 58 ff.*]. This was the same time that Communists took over in Hungary (March to August), and the leaders of the Hungarian Soviet regime were also overwhelmingly Jewish. The prospect of the spread of 'Red terror' from Russia to Germany, of the 'Jewish' Bolsheviks in Russia violently taking over his beloved fatherland, seems to have been both appalling and unbearable for Hitler.

There is evidence that Hitler first attracted wide attention and felt some glimmering of his oratorical powers when, again in 1919, he attacked a speaker who was defending the Jews; the applause he received from the crowd may be seen as psychologically as well as programmatically important. He had, finally at the age of thirty, engaged himself publicly in the struggle against the Jews. He began to associate with anti-Semitic activists and to be attacked by those who opposed the anti-Semites. These processes had their own radicalizing logic in terms of pushing an already stiff and prickly young Hitler toward a more angry, dogmatic, and 'uncompromising' stance.

In other ways, too, these experiences in 1919 may have played in decisive ways upon aspects of Hitler's peculiar personality. One of his boyhood friends remarked that even in his teens Hitler was headstrong, proud, and a bundle of hostilities. Another who knew him commented that 'he seemed always to feel the need for something to hate.' Hitler himself, in one of many passages in *Mein Kampf* that seem to reveal more about his own personality than he intended, wrote that the masses are best organized by hatred; a leader of the masses must simplify and exaggerate, not confuse the people with nuances and qualifications. 'The only stable emotion is hatred' [108 *p. 492*]. It was true for him – why not for others?

One can speculate that Hitler's gross simplifications and public demonization of the Jews may initially have had a pragmatic or simply manipulative aspect, that he himself may not have hated the Jews in such a simplistic or sweeping fashion as his public statements seem to indicate. Such speculation is supported by a number of private comments he made, including those that ridiculed the simplemindedness of the party's radical anti-Semites. His curt refusal, on the other hand, to discuss the matter with those among his closer contacts who offered even limited defenses of the Jews may be seen as another indication of his inner uncertainties, masked by bluster and arrogance.

If there was process and ambiguity in Hitler's move toward an intensely demonized view of the Jews, it is also plausible that his precise program for Jews emerged only over a lengthy period and in relation to his power to put his ideas into action. Could the Hitler of 1929 really have imagined the vast power he would have by 1939, or indeed the number of Jews under his power once Nazi Germany had expanded eastward and taken over those territories where the majority of the Jews of the world lived?

If the old adage that power corrupts and absolute power corrupts absolutely has any validity, there would seem to be no better example than Hitler. One of his acquaintances in the 1920s later wrote that 'it was the experience of power which finally turned Hitler into an irreconcilable fanatic' [68 *pp. 224–5*]. Hitler's degenerating health after 1933 – he aged rapidly, brooded constantly about a premature death, and probably suffered from Parkinson's disease (which when untreated is characterized in its later stages by dementia) – may have further inclined him to psychic disintegration and moral chaos. That such a man became one of the most powerful and revered leaders in history is a key to the tragedies that were to follow. But that story is for another volume.

THE 'SWEET EXILES'

Any history of anti-Semitism risks, by the nature of the enterprise, exaggerating the importance or pervasiveness of Jew-hatred. The description and analysis of it in these pages has noted that throughout history Jews did not encounter hostility everywhere they settled. Indeed, Jewish survival over the centuries and millennia is inconceivable if Jews had been hated as much as some believe. The situation of Jews in Italy in the late nineteenth and early twentieth centuries is one example of what has been called a 'sweet exile' (Hebrew: *galut metuka*). To be sure, Jews who had so enthusiastically opted for Italian nationality learned in the late 1930s that their fidelities were tragically ill-placed. A similar story holds for the Jews of Hungary, who from the mid-nineteenth century up to 1914 participated brilliantly in Hungarian culture, as well as becoming extremely important economically and politically. But that era of highly successful integration was followed by one of sometimes fierce anti-Semitism, after the Hungarian Communist regime took over in 1919.

In both the Italian and Hungarian cases, the relatively low levels of anti-Semitism in the nineteenth and early twentieth centuries can be related to the perception of the non-Jewish population that their Jewish fellow citizens were useful to and supportive of them, not alien or destructive. These 'good/bad' examples of Jewish–Gentile relationships can be revealingly compared to examples that were more lastingly positive, the Jewish experience in the English-speaking world, most notably in Britain and the United States. While hostility to Jews certainly existed in those countries, it was relatively weak and of less political relevance throughout the modern period. Indeed, it might be more fitting to write a history of philo-Semitism than of anti-Semitism in the modern histories of Britain and the United States [149].

Those two countries were unusually prosperous and were mostly on the winning side – in a variety of senses beyond the obvious military one – in modern times. The noted British (and Jewish) historian Lewis Namier wrote that 'two races headed the movement of modernity ... the British and the Jews; they were the pioneers of capitalism and its first, perhaps chief beneficiaries' [170 *pp. 84–5*]. Jewish populations were extremely small in both Britain and the United States in the eighteenth and early nineteenth centuries, when those two countries began to industrialize, and thus Jews could not be closely associated with (or blamed for) that process.

The rise of capitalism has been associated with Protestantism as well as Judaism; in Protestant Britain money, banking, and commercial enterprise became identified with Christians, especially in London. Elsewhere, especially in central and eastern Europe, Jews rather than Christians were prominent as bankers and merchants. The growth of parliament and the rule of law also had favorable implications for Jews. Monarchies that typically granted Jews privileges and protections were the norm on the Continent, whereas parliament did no such thing, nor did any modern British king. For these and other reasons, Jews in Britain were not widely considered to be either a privileged or politically subversive group [147 *pp. 42–3*].

Many of the same points in the economic realm can be made about Jews in America, with the further important point that in America there was not much of a feudal past to cast off; Jews had not been put into separate legal categories, at least not on a national level. There were laws in some states that discriminated against Jews, especially in the eighteenth and early part of the nineteenth centuries, but Jews never faced the same degree of legal ostracism or social separatism that they did in Europe.

When the numbers of Jews coming from Europe began to rise rapidly in both Britain and the United States, from the 1880s on, anti-Semitism became a more significant issue. In the United States, after World War I various anti-Semitic demagogues, such as Henry Ford [*Doc. 14*] and Father Coughlin, gained unprecedented visibility, but there was never much likelihood that laws depriving Jews of their rights as citizens would be passed or large-scale violence against them initiated.

As elsewhere, Jewish–Gentile tensions in Britain and the United States became most notable in periods of general crisis, but anti-Jewish flare-ups remained on a far less significant scale than elsewhere. Americans, 'the people of plenty,' enjoying secure borders and unparalleled material prosperity, experienced fewer major crises than did most Europeans in modern times. Britain, too, as 'the workshop of the world' and the widely acknowledged model of modern industrial expansion, enjoyed growing material comfort and political stability for much of the period from the mid-nineteenth century to 1914. The distinguished historian John Higham has written that in America 'no decisive event, no deep crisis, no powerful social movement, no great individual is associated primarily ... with anti-Semitism' [108 *p. 253*].

A sense of difference did remain. The twentieth-century British politician, Austen Chamberlain, expressed an opinion that paralleled those often made in regard to Disraeli: 'A Jew may be a loyal Englishman ... but he is intellectually apart from us and will never be purely and simply English' [147 *p. 207*]. Mark Twain made similar remarks a half-century earlier. It was no surprise to him that Jews were often disliked, since the Jew 'is substantially a foreigner wherever he may be, and even the angels dislike a foreigner' [108 *p. 377*]. Very few members of the British and American elites, however, had any use for political and racial anti-Semitism; Austen Chamberlain was a firm anti-Nazi and Mark Twain was recognized by Jews as a friend.

The social exclusion suffered by Jews in English-speaking countries could be cruel and psychologically searing, but it nonetheless did not seem to deter Jewish achievement in many realms in the nineteenth century. Such must finally even be said about the eastern European Jews, for all their greater numbers (by the 1920s over 90 percent of Jews in America were of eastern European origin), cultural differences, and initial poverty. Whatever the obstacles they faced, most Jews in America and Britain continued to nourish hopes for the future, at least for their children. Similarly, non-Jews in America and Britain retained significant degrees of sympathy and admiration for Jews. For all the tempestuous shifts in public opinion about Jews, over the long run it appears that most British and American non-Jews concluded that Jewish differences were tolerable and that Jews were decidedly more beneficial than harmful.

The rise of the Jews in Britain and America in the nineteenth century was less spectacular and less noticed than in Germany and other areas of central Europe, although in the twentieth century that rise, especially in America from the 1930s onward, has been in some regards comparable to the rise in nineteenth-century Europe. Traditions of toleration, liberal institutions, and common commercial identities all help to explain the relative lack of anti-Semitism even when Jews rose rapidly, but probably most important has been the near absence of major economic and social crises, linked to the fact that during the period of greatest crisis for Britain and the United States, national identity assumed a strongly anti-Nazi tone. Once at war against Nazi Germany, American and British citizens naturally reaffirmed their opposition to anti-Semitism, although no doubt many unfavorable opinions about Jews lingered. Revulsion from the Holocaust, as its dimensions became known, only added to the tendency to see anti-Semitism as particularly dangerous and barbaric. Jewish 'difference' and the remarkable upward mobility of Jews make them vulnerable to resentment, but in the foreseeable future a recurrence of the hostilities of the 1930s appears highly unlikely.

CONCLUSION

The Introduction began with the question of whether anti-Semitism can be understood, while the final chapter returned to the question in a more pointed form by asking if one can understand the anti-Semite of all anti-Semites, Hitler. If we are speaking of perfect understanding, the answer to both questions must be No. However, that does not mean that we are pushed to the opposite extreme, to the conclusion that efforts to understand anti-Semitism are unacceptably dangerous because of the sometimes unsettling ways that understanding and sympathy tend to intertwine. Similarly, it is not unacceptably perilous, in a moral sense, to ask why a man like Treitschke lashed out at the Jews of his day, or indeed why it was that Churchill made comments about Jews that today would be denounced as shockingly anti-Semitic.

I have taken the position in these pages that it is inadequate to dismiss such people as simply corrupt morally and hopelessly in the grips of baseless fantasies; Treitschke and Churchill had reasons for making anti-Jewish statements that we can understand – indeed feel sympathy for – even if in retrospect, knowing things they did not, we judge those reasons to have been flawed. For people who search history in order to place historical actors into boxes labeled 'good guys' and 'bad guys,' the label 'anti-Semite' may satisfy in application to those two European nationalists, but most of us will find such pigeon-holing unsatisfactory. We might well conclude that this kind of reasoning is finally 'bad for the Jews' – and for everyone else – because of the way that it embraces a black-and-white manner of thinking that has much in common with that of the anti-Semites.

I find it unsatisfactory to conceptualize the history of anti-Semitism as an elaborate catalogue of hostile things said about and done to Jews, in which Jews themselves implicitly remain passive, unengaged objects, without character, initiative, or responsibility. I have tried to conceptualize both Jews and non-Jews as active agents in history.

Both of them have formed ideas about one another through an elusive dialectic of inherited prejudice and ever-refreshed observation. My approach suggests that we look critically at such familiar phrases as 'blaming the victim,' hating Jews 'for no reason,' or persecuting Jews 'just because they were Jews.' These phrases are often uttered without serious reflection about what they might mean or their more subtle implications. I also suggest that the allegedly integral connections of Christian beliefs and the Holocaust have often been overstated, as indeed have those between racism and Jew-hatred. Even anti-Semitism and the Holocaust have a less simple relationship to one another than is widely believed.

Serious attention has been paid in these pages to objective factors as well as fantasies, to economic and social data as well as religious beliefs and modern ideologies, in explaining group conflicts. It is by no means basically irrelevant, when seeking to understand outbreaks of anti-Semitism, to know the percentage of Jews in a given population or the nature and character of those Jews, their wealth, social position, rates of ascent, language, culture, attitudes to non-Jews. Such concrete data must of course be scrutinized with care, but attention to such information opens the possibility of reasonably informed scholarly exchanges, rather than one-sided tendentious narratives that pretend to be providing 'just the facts.'

Such narratives, common in the literature on anti-Semitism, are characterized by a number of interrelated problems. Chapter 1 explored how incoherent, finally baffling the images of the 'enemies of Israel' in premodern times have often been. It is tempting to conclude that those deeply embedded yet garbled images have worked in unconscious ways to undermine many modern efforts to conceptualize Jew-hatred. A satisfactory model can hardly be derived from Esau's all too understandable hatred for Jacob. We cannot conclude that the modern anti-Semite's hatred of Jews was like that of Esau's anger toward Jacob's devious efforts to disinherit him. Pharaoh's actions offer a scarcely less awkward model for modern observers, unless one accepts that the Holocaust and other outbreaks of anti-Semitism were directed by God for mystical purposes or to punish His people.

Haman offers a more engaging model from a modern standpoint, in part because the Book of Esther leaves God or divine purposes out of the picture. In that book we encounter tribalism, inherited hatred requiring no immediate or palpable cause, as the reason Haman plotted to murder Jews. Still, there is also the fact that Mordecai insulted Haman in a flagrant and apparently unprovoked way –

starting things, as it were – and making Haman's anger understand-able. Mordecai's motives for the insult remain obscure but ostensibly also reflected tribalistic attitudes. Further complicating matters, the Jewish people in the Book of Esther lead a shadowy existence, lacking any notable moral dimension, any clearly asserted association with the one true god and his superior morality. Haman denounces the Jews as 'different' but does not say much about the nature of that difference, and it is not immediately obvious from the bare text why Mordecai and his tribe should be ranked morally above Haman and his or any others in the kingdom. A reader who is innocent of the symbolic significance of the links of Mordecai to Saul and Haman to Amalek might well see the tale as an all too familiar one of two tribes seething with inherited hatred and ready to murder one another on the slightest pretext. Such a reader might even conclude that the Jews, by ostensibly refusing to respect the laws of the state (we are not told which laws are at issue or how they were being disobeyed), were the kind of disloyal or subversive element that any ruler must view with suspicion. Here as elsewhere in the Bible, interpretation is all im-portant, bare text dangerously prone to 'incorrect' interpretation.

The charges that Christians brought against the Jews, although in some regards similar to earlier accusations that Jews were dangerous dissidents, or diseased corrupters, moved into territory that may be termed qualitatively different. Jews were described not only as dissident but perversely – outrageously and incomprehensibly – so. They reviled, tortured, and murdered God's Son. And they have harbored, in the centuries after that cosmic crime, a seething hatred of Christian universalistic ideals. They have similarly detested the followers of Christ, secretly tormenting and ritually executing them, especially innocent Christian children. This peculiar demonization of the Jews, derived from religious myths of a shocking, graphic nature, seems to have allowed a peculiar quality of Jew-hatred to sink into the hearts of many Christians.

Nonetheless, Christian attitudes to Jews were characterized over the centuries by much diversity and relatively little violence. It was not until Jews in Europe began to be widely and plausibly associated with threatening activities in the real world, especially with money-lending and with 'rising' beyond the level that was judged permissible for people living under a divine curse, that large-scale, endemic violence against them began to occur. Christian doctrine alone, even if encouraging the growth of self-perpetuating fantasies of a horrific sort, remained for a thousand years ostensibly not enough in itself to provoke bloodshed of recurrent, major dimensions.

This long history of relative peace was due in no small part to the fact that Christian doctrine explicitly set down that Jews were not to be physically attacked or forced to convert. Indeed, Christianity lastingly retained a somewhat contradictory philo-Semitic potential, realized most notably in a few varieties of Protestantism. Moreover, it seems that in all periods, from ancient to modern, many Jews and Christians continued to recognize a human face in one another, in a practical or common-sense way, however much elements of their respective religions encouraged hatred and revulsion of others.

The anti-Christian Jew-hatred of the Enlightenment rejected deicide and its associated fantasies but returned to the older charges that Jews were intolerant, hide-bound, and destructively contempt-uous of others. Jews themselves were denounced as the originators of the very religious intolerance that the Christians, fancying themselves the 'true Jews,' had turned against the Jews. But Voltaire's distaste and ridicule were qualified in important ways, especially by stressing that whatever the failings of the Jews, 'we should not burn them.' He had conciliatory, friendly words for individual Jews who seemed to be casting off Jewish intolerance. Similarly, the willingness of many of the deputies to the French National Assembly, in the debates of 1789–91, to accept civil equality for the Sephardim while resisting it for the Ashkenazim suggests that what was bothering them was not 'just because [the Ashkenazim] were Jews' but specific antisocial qualities associated with given elements of the Jewish population at that time.

A final and important difference between Christian and Enlight-ened viewpoints may be seen in the fact that philo-Semitism was expressed, most famously in the writings of Lessing, with unprece-dented boldness and visibility by the late eighteenth century. In the next hundred years, the common humanity as well as the civil equality of Jews were formally recognized by most of Europe's states, matched by a growing willingness on the part of Jews to distance themselves from the hostile imagery in regard to non-Jews that their religious tradition had retained. Similarly, philo-Semitism became more important, both among Christians and secularists. On the other hand, the older attitudes lingered on, assuming what now appear portentously dangerous new forms.

The most prominent racial-political anti-Semites of the 1880s to 1914 in western and central Europe did not call for violence but rather legal measures to counter what they perceived as a precipitous and threatening rise of the Jews. But, revealingly, their panicked perceptions were not shared by a large enough part of the population to allow any anti-Semitic laws to be passed. Of course in 'medieval'

Russia, where anti-Jewish legislation continued to pile up in the course of the century, the laws were not the result of popular votes but were rather based on the edicts of the tsar. But this anti-Jewish legislation had something in common with what was being proposed in the west, that is, to exercise vigilant control of Russia's Jewish subjects, especially since they were perceived as rapidly expanding in numbers and in other ways threatening the nature of tsarist rule and Christian society.

Modern secular hostility to Jews significantly lacked the Christian belief that Jewish survival was part of God's plan. Many non-Jewish secularists did comment that Jews added spice to life; a number of non-Jews expressed a belief that Jews were unusually idealistic, intellectually gifted, and artistically creative. In short, Jews were recognized by such observers as useful rather than detrimental to society in general. And the great majority of non-Jews opposed persecution of Jews. Even anti-Semites like Marr condemned past Christian persecution. Nonetheless, most modern secular observers implicitly anticipated a time when Jews would 'disappear,' when they would willingly blend into a common humanity. Obviously, anticipations of that sort were vastly different from desiring the murder of all Jews. Only a peculiarly modern sense of being able to solve all problems through the powers of the state – moral considerations to the wind – could lead toward such monstrous measures as finally taken by the Nazis.

At any rate, the term 'bloodless holocaust,' used by some Orthodox Jewish observers to describe the voluntary decision of millions of Jews in modern times to abandon traditional Jewish identity and thus 'die' must be described as unfortunate if not offensive. It is only slightly less so when such observers as Harvard Law School professor and famous trial lawyer, Alan Dershowitz, speak of Jews in modern times being 'seduced' away from their Jewishness, as distinguished from their being 'raped' in previous times [39 *pp. 353–4*].

There certainly were secularists, before 1914 and before Hitler, who spoke in terms that implied anti-Jewish violence (e.g., Proudhon, Dühring, Lagarde). However, their genocidal musings about Jews won far fewer admirers than did the proposals to return to a period of limited Jewish civil rights, and, again, even those proposals won over only a small minority of the population. The secularism associated with these Jew-haters, and in particular the way that moral limits in regard to Jews tended to disappear in the ideologies they advocated, must be considered an important part of the explanation of how men like Hitler could move in the murderous directions they did. But still decidedly more influential were the limitless visions of mass murder that had been provided in World War I and Communist Russia. Even if the anti-Semitism of many Nazis derived in part from Christian habits of mind, their lack of a sense of moral limits – their belief that 'anything is permitted' – must be more closely linked to the experiences of totalitarian warfare, the mad utopias of right and left, and the demented social engineering that emerged from modern ideologies and the dynamics of modernization. A systematic physical destruction of all Jews was not a program of ancient Greek or Roman rulers, nor of Christian thinkers, nor of Europe's political leaders, including the tsars of Russia. To be sure, a few Christian figures – Luther comes immediately to mind – did speak in terms that suggested radical, violent action against the Jews. But again there was little follow-through to their rhetoric, no systematic application of it, and much revulsion from it by other Christian leaders, many of whom, to be sure, were at the same time no particular friends of the Jews.

Justifications for mass murder, at any rate, might never have come into play if Europe had not undergone, between 1914 and 1939, repeated and unparalleled disasters in the material world. That Europe's most catastrophic time of troubles overlapped the most impressive rise of the Jews in history made for an ominous and horrific combination. That such typically modern ideologies as liberalism, capitalism and Communism exercised special appeals to Jews and were plausibly linked to them must similarly be taken into consideration when trying to explain the appeals of modern anti-Semitism.

Those same developments, however, contributed to the respect and indeed adulation that many Jews have enjoyed in modern times; the competing negative and positive images cannot be separated, since the admiration of Jews by some was an important part of the reason that others so hated and feared Jews. Those first arrested in large numbers by the Nazi regime were Communists and Socialists, not Jews as such, but in fact disproportionately Jews because of the large role Jews played in those two movements. Indeed, the majority of the Jews arrested in the first years of the Nazi regime were left-wingers, ostensibly arrested for their political convictions rather than their Jewish origin.

For all the obvious importance of broad, impersonal forces, it is impossible to ignore the role of individuals in the working out of the history of anti-Semitism. Hitler's personality, his will, the unquestioning devotion to him of so many Germans are absolutely essential elements of any explanation of the Nazi period and especially the final tragedies of the years 1939–45. Indeed, Hitler's personality seems to have been an essential element to the functioning of the totalitarian Nazi state itself, in that the chaotically and ruthlessly competing agencies of that state constantly vied for his approval, in issues as diverse as foreign policy, economic planning, and the 'final solution' to the Jewish question.

The rivalry of those agencies made for an ever-radicalizing dynamic in Nazi Germany, trapping Jews and others in the monstrous dynamic of totalitarianism. In that regard, it is food for thought that the first to be systematically murdered were not Jews but the mentally and physically handicapped. Similarly, Gypsies were slated for mass murder alongside the Jews. Yet anti-Gypsy or anti-handicapped ideology can hardly be considered 'longest hatreds,' 'rising tides,' or major long-range themes of western civilization. If the Nazi state had not been defeated in warfare, it is likely that other opponents or perceived enemies would eventually have been slated for mass destruction by it.

The notion of a mass, systematic destruction of the Jews stood outside the main themes of European history prior to 1914. Jewish–Gentile relations have by no means been only a history of hatred, and in modern times those relations have not been characterized by a clearly discernible rising tide of hatred pointing toward mass destruction. Over hundreds of years Jews and non-Jews in Europe and America have influenced one another in ways that cannot be reduced to black and white categories, or to self-contained fantasies.

It is all too tempting to reason that since the Holocaust was carried out by Germans there must have been in German history a hatred that gathered inexorably until it finally found expression in mass murder. There is certainly some evidence to support such reasoning, but it is finally unpersuasive. If one sets out to write a history of anti-Semitism by looking only for hatred, it can easily be found. But there is also more to the story.

The issue of the power is central. For most of the past two thousand years, Jews have been weak and their adversaries strong, but even in that regard one must avoid unwarranted simplifications. Jews have exercised various kinds of influence and power, although obviously not the kind of clandestine-demonic power that their most inflamed enemies have charged. And when Jews have too visibly or rapidly 'risen,' they have not surprisingly encountered a similarly rising consternation and hostility, based to a significant degree on fantasy but nourished also by accurate perceptions.

However, I have been careful to point out that the mere fact of a Jewish rise is not in itself adequate to explain hatred of Jews in all its diversity, range of intensity, and irrationality. There have been countries in which Jews have risen while relative harmony between Jews and non-Jews has prevailed for significant periods. And just as hostility needs to be understood in terms of an interplay between fantasy and reality, so does harmony: it makes little sense to argue that Jews have been hated only for fantastic reasons but admired only for real reasons. Liberal or philo-Semitic visions of the Jews have not been free of their own kinds of fantasy; Lessing's admirable Nathan must be considered as much an artistic invention as Dickens's detestable Fagin (the Jew in *Oliver Twist*). But more generally and palpably, when the presence of Jews has been considered beneficial, hostility to them has been relatively unimportant; when they are perceived as threatening, the likelihood of hostility increases. It is too easy to assert that in these contrasting images – as, say, in the United States compared to Russia – the differences were only the result of the different fantasies of the dominant peoples and had absolutely nothing to do with genuine conflicts over real interests and identities.

In a similar way, it is not only ignorance about Jews that has fed fear and hatred of them. The familiar remark that anti-Semitism often exists without Jews being present is true, but it is often overdone, since obviously people who have had no knowledge of Jews whatso-ever – the Jivaro Indians or the Inuit, let us say – have not been anti-Semites. Even the bizarre forms of anti-Semitism that have appeared in Japan, where there has been no significant Jewish presence in history, has much to do with a Japanese belief in the power of Jews internationally. Similarly, Polish anti-Semitism after the Holocaust has had to do with both pre-existing anti-Semitism and the perception of many Poles that although Jews are no longer present in significant numbers inside Poland, they still have much influence in other countries, especially the United States, often to the detriment of Poland's image in the world.

It must be re-emphasized that open-minded efforts to understand anti-Semites do not lead inexorably to sympathy for them. One can understand why a murder has been committed without concluding that the murderer was not guilty and should be set free. Similarly, although anti-Semites have insisted that their hatred is based on reality, not fantasy, it is not at all the case that recognition of the role of realistic perceptions in the emergence of Jew-hatred then un-avoidably grants the anti-Semites their major point. These pages have abundantly recognized the crucial role of fantasy but at the same time insisted that fantasy and reality need to be conceptually synthesized. Anti-Americanism often takes the form of crude caricatures based on ignorance, but Americans would be ill-advised to conclude that dislike of them is in all instances utterly divorced from reality and can thus be discounted.

Does history over the centuries and millennia demonstrate that anti-Semitism is endemic, in some sense inevitable, even in such 'sweet exiles' as the United States and Britain? Given the number of examples in history when harmony between Jew and non-Jew has turned into discord, it would be naïve to say 'it cannot happen here.' So long as Jews cultivate a separate identity – particularly with the many traditional associations of that identity – a potential for new outbreaks of hatred will continue to exist. But they are hardly inevitable. Outbreaks of anti-Semitism, even if not entirely predictable, can nonetheless be anticipated, prepared for, and in some instances prevented by cooperative, reasonable actions by both non-Jews and Jews. At the same time, there remains much that we do not and probably never will understand about Jew-hatred. Hopes to prevent future outbreaks must be joined by sober realism.

DOCUMENTS

These source readings should provide a more in-depth and nuanced sense of points made in the main text. Students should look for continuities in the images of Jews, both negative (conniving, exploitative, destructive, alien) and positive (intelligent, creative, highly moral, useful), and of course ambiguous mixes of the two. For the most part, these texts represent statements made by influential figures and point to major themes of anti-Semitism over the ages.

DOCUMENT 1   JACOB AND ESAU, JEW AND NON-JEW

Isaac was forty years old when he took to wife Rebekah. ... And Isaac prayed to the Lord for his wife, because she was barren; and the Lord granted his prayer, and Rebekah his wife conceived. The children struggled together within her; and she said, 'If it is thus, why do I live?' So she went to inquire of the Lord. And the Lord said to her:

Two nations are in your womb, and two peoples, born of you, shall be divided; the one shall be stronger than the other, and the elder shall serve the younger.

When her days to be delivered were fulfilled, behold, there were twins in her womb. The first came forth red, all his body like a hairy mantle; so they called his name Esau. Afterward his brother came forth, and his hand had taken ahold of Esau's heel; so his name was called Jacob. Isaac was sixty years old when she bore them.

When the boys grew up, Esau was a skilful hunter, a man of the field, while Jacob was a quiet man, dwelling in the tents. Isaac loved Esau, because he ate his game; but Rebekah loved Jacob.

Once when Jacob was boiling pottage, Esau came in from the field, and he was famished. And Esau said to Jacob, 'Let me eat some of that red pottage, for I am famished!' ... Jacob said, 'First sell me your birthright.' And Esau said, 'I am about to die; of what use is my birthright to me?' Jacob said, 'Swear to me first.' So he swore to him, and sold his birthright to Jacob. Then

Jacob gave Esau bread and pottage of lentils and went his way. Thus Esau despised his birthright. [Birthright entailed leadership of the family and a double share of the inheritance.] ...

When Isaac was old and his eyes were dim so that he could not see, he called Esau his older son, and said to him, 'My son,' and he answered 'Here I am.' He said, 'Behold, I am old; I do not know the day of my death. Now, then, take your weapons, your quiver and your bow, and go out into the field, and hunt game for me, and prepare for me the savory food, such as I love, and bring it to me that I may eat; that I may bless you before I die.'

Now Rebekah was listening when Isaac spoke to his son Esau. So when Esau went to the field to hunt for game and bring it, Rebekah said to her son Jacob, 'I heard your father speak to your brother Esau, "Bring me game and prepare for me savory food, that I may eat it, and bless you before I die." Now, therefore, my son, obey my word as I command you. Go to the flock, and fetch two good kids, that I may prepare from them savory food, such as your father loves; and you shall bring it to your father to eat, so that he may bless you before he dies.' But Jacob said to Rebekah his mother, 'Behold, my brother Esau is a hairy man, and I am a smooth man. Perhaps my father will feel me, and I shall seem to be mocking him, and bring a curse upon myself and not a blessing.' His mother said to him, 'Upon me be your curse, my son; only obey my word, and go, fetch them to me.' So he went and took them and brought them to his mother; and his mother prepared savory food, such as his father loved.

Then Rebekah took the best garments of Esau, her elder son, which were with her in the house, and put them on Jacob her younger son; and the skins of the kids she put upon his hands and upon the smooth part of his neck; and she gave the savory food, and the bread, which she had prepared, into the hand of her son Jacob.

So he went in to his father, and said, 'My father'; and he said 'Here I am; who are you, my son?' Jacob said to his father, 'I am Esau your first-born, and I have done as you told me; now sit up and eat of my game, that you may bless me.' But Isaac said to his son, 'How is it that you have found it so quickly, my son?' He answered, 'Because the Lord your God granted me success'. Then Isaac said to Jacob, 'Come near, that I may feel you, my son, to know whether you are really my son Esau or not.' So Jacob went near to Isaac his father, who felt him and said, 'The voice is Jacob's voice, but the hands are the hands of Esau.' And he did not recognize him, because his hands were hairy like his brother Esau's hands; so he blessed him. He said, 'Are you really my son Esau?' He answered, 'I am.' Then he said, 'Bring it to me, that I may eat of my son's game and bless you.' So he brought it to him, and he ate; and he brought him wine, and he drank. Then his father, Isaac, said to him, 'Come near and kiss me, my son.' So he came near and kissed him; and he smelled the smell of his garments, and blessed him, and said,

See, the smell of my son is the smell of a field in which the Lord has blessed! May God give you of the dew of heaven, and of the fatness of the earth, and plenty of grain and wine. Let peoples serve you, and nations bow down to you. Be Lord over your brothers, and may your mother's sons bow down to you. Cursed be everyone who curses you, and blessed be everyone who blesses you!

As soon as Isaac had finished blessing Jacob, when Jacob had scarcely gone out from the presence of Isaac his father, Esau his brother came in from hunting. He also prepared savory food and brought it to his father. And he said to his father, 'Let my father arise, and eat of his son's game, that you may bless me.' His father Isaac said to him, 'Who are you?' He answered, 'I am your son, your first-born, Esau.' Then Isaac trembled violently and said, 'Who was it then who hunted game and brought it to me ... and I have blessed him?' ...

When Esau heard the words of his father, he cried out with an exceedingly great and bitter cry, and said to his father, 'Bless me, even also, O my father!' But he said, 'Your brother came with guile, and he has taken away your blessing.' Esau said, 'Is he not rightly called Jacob? For he has supplanted me these two times. He took away my birthright, and behold, now he has taken away my blessing.' Then he said, 'Have you not reserved a blessing for me?' ....

Then Isaac his father answered him:

... By your sword shall you live, and you shall serve your brother; but when you break loose, you shall break his yoke from your neck.

Now Esau hated Jacob ... and Esau said to himself, 'The days of mourning for my father are approaching; then will I kill my brother Jacob.'

From Genesis, chapters 25: 19–26; 26 and 27, *Revised Standard Version of the Bible*, New York, 1973.

DOCUMENT 2   A ROMAN HISTORIAN'S ACCOUNT OF THE ORIGINS OF THE JEWS

Tacitus (57–117 AD), was a celebrated and influential Roman historian. His account obviously borrowed from Manetho or other Egyptian sources and helped to perpetuate views expressed in them.

Most writers agree ... in stating that once a disease, which horribly disfigured the body, broke out over Egypt; that king Bocchoris, in seeking a remedy, consulted the oracle of Hammon, and was bidden to cleanse his realm, and to convey to some foreign land this race detested by the gods. The [Jewish] people ... finding themselves left in a desert, sat for the most part in a stupor of grief, until one of the exiles, Moyses by name, warned them not to look for any relief from God or man ... but to trust to themselves, taking for their heaven-sent leader that man who should first help them to be quit of their present misery. ...

Moyses, wishing to secure for the future his authority over the nation, gave them a novel form of worship, opposed to all that is practiced by other men. Things sacred with us, with them have no sanctity, while they allow what with us is forbidden. In their holy place they have consecrated an image of the animal [an ass] by whose guidance they found deliverance from their long and thirsty wanderings. They ... sacrifice the ox because the Egyptians worship it as Apis. They abstain from swine's flesh, in consideration of what they suffered when they were infected with the leprosy to which this animal is still liable. ...

[The Jews] sit apart at meals, they sleep apart, and though, as a nation, they are singularly prone to lust, they abstain from intercourse with foreign women; among themselves nothing is unlawful. Circumcision was adopted by them as a mark of difference from other men.

From *The Annals and the Histories*, Book V; reprinted in Adler, [2], p. 295.

DOCUMENT 3   'CONCERNING THE JEWS AND THEIR LIES' (1543)

Martin Luther (1483–1546) led the Protestant Reformation. Initially, he made sympathetic overtures to the Jews, but when those overtures were rebuffed, his sympathy turned into bitter hatred.

What then shall we Christians do with this damned, rejected race of Jews? Since they live among us and we know about their lying and blasphemy and cursing, we cannot tolerate them if we do not wish to share in their lies, curses, and blasphemy. In this way we cannot quench the inextinguishable fire of divine rage (as the prophets say) nor convert the Jews. We must prayerfully and reverentially practice a merciful severity. Perhaps we may save a few from the fire and the flames. We must not seek vengeance. They are surely being punished a thousand times more than we might wish them. Let me give you my honest advice.

First, their synagogues ... should be set on fire, and whatever does not burn up should be covered ... with dirt, so that no one may ever be able to see a cinder or stone of it. ...

Secondly, their homes should likewise be broken down and destroyed. ... [T]hey ought to be put under one roof or a stable, like gypsies, in order that they may realize that they are not masters in our land, as they boast, but miserable captives. ...

Thirdly, they should be deprived of their prayer books and Talmuds, in which such idolatry, lies, cursing, and blasphemy are taught.

Fourthly, their rabbis must be forbidden under threat of death to teach any more. ...

Fifthly, ... traveling privileges should be absolutely forbidden to the Jews. ...

Sixthly, they ought to be stopped from usury. All their cash and valuables of silver and gold ought to be taken from them and put aside for safe keeping. ...

Seventhly, let the young and strong Jews and Jewesses be given the flail, the ax, the hoe, the spade, the distaff, the spindle, and let them earn their bread by the sweat of their noses, as is enjoined upon Adam's children. For it is not proper that they should want us cursed Goyyim to work in the sweat of our brow, and that they, pious crew, idle away their days at the fireside in laziness, feasting, and display. ...

To sum up, dear princes and nobles who have Jews in your domains, if this advice of mine does not suit you, then find a better one so that you and we may be free of this insufferable devilish burden – the Jews.

From A. Gould, [62], pp. 51–2.

DOCUMENT 4   'HOW PROFITABLE THE NATION OF THE JEWS ARE' (1655)

Menasseh ben Israel (c. 1604–57) was a Dutch rabbi of Sephardic origin, an older contemporary of Spinoza. His petition makes an interesting comparison with the words of Luther, some hundred years earlier, and suggests how little Luther's recommendations were carried out by the princes he addressed. Note how this author defines the Jewish nation; there is no question yet of Jews being citizens equal under the law. The archaic wording and orthography have been altered in a few places.

Three things ... make a strange nation well beloved among the natives of a land where they dwell: the profit they may receive from them; the fidelity they hold toward their princes; and their nobleness and purity of blood. ... All three things are found in the Jewish nation.

Profit is the most powerful motive, which all the world prefers before all other things. ... Merchandizing is the proper profession of the nation of the Jews. Having banished them from their own country, God has given them a natural instinct, by which they might not only gain what is necessary for their need but that they shall also thrive in riches and possessions, and thus they become not only gracious to their princes and lords but are invited by others to come and dwell in their lands. ... There arises an infallible profit, commodity, and gain to all those princes in whose lands they dwell. ...

In Germany, there live ... a great multitude of Jews, especially at Prague, Vienna, and Frankfurt, very much favored by the most mild and most gracious emperors, but despised by the people. ... But yet a greater number of Jews are found in the Kingdom of Poland, Prussia, and Lithuania, under which monarchy they have the jurisdiction to judge amongst themselves all causes, both criminal and civil, and also great and famous academies of their own. ... Although the Cossacks in the late wars killed more than one hundred and eighty thousand of them, yet it is sustained that they are yet at this day as innumerable as those were that came out of Egypt. In that kingdom, the whole negotiation [commerce] is in the hands of the Jews. The remaining Christians are either noblemen or peasants kept as slaves. ...

So we see that if one prince, ill-advised, drives the Jews out of his land, yet another invites them into his. Wherein we may see the prophesy fulfilled to the letter: 'The staff (to support him) shall not depart from Jacob, until Messiah comes.' And this prophesy shall suffice concerning the value of the Jewish nation.

From Mendes-Flohr and Reinharz, [122], pp. 10–13.

DOCUMENT 5   AN EIGHTEENTH-CENTURY HISTORIAN'S
VIEW OF THE JEWS IN ANCIENT TIMES

This passage from Edward Gibbon's history of the fall of the Roman Empire illustrates attitudes similar to those of Voltaire and, more remotely, Tacitus.

We have already described the religious harmony of the ancient world, and the facility with which the most different and even hostile nations embraced, or at least respected, each other's superstitions. A single people refused to join in the common intercourse of mankind. The Jews, who, under the Assyrian and Persian monarchies, had languished for many ages as the most despised portion of their slaves, emerged from obscurity under the successors of Alexander; and as they multiplied to a surprising degree in the East, and afterwards in the West, they soon excited the curiosity and wonder of other nations. The sullen obstinacy with which they maintained their peculiar rites and unsocial manners seemed to mark them out as a distinct species of men, who boldly professed, or who faintly disguised, their implacable hatred to the rest of human-kind. Neither the violence of Antiochus ... nor the example of the [surrounding] nations, could ever persuade the Jews to associate the institutions of Moses with the elegant mythology of the Greeks. According to the maxims of universal toleration, the Romans protected a superstition which they despised. ... But the moderation of the conquerors was insufficient to appease the jealous prejudices of these subjects. ... Their attachment to the Law of Moses was equal to their detestation of foreign religions. ...

From Adler, [2], pp. 179–80.

DOCUMENT 6 'AN ESSAY ON THE PHYSICAL, MORAL, AND POLITICAL REFORMATION OF THE JEWS' (1789)

The remarks of Abbé Henri Baptiste Grégoire (1750–1834), which were at the time considered favorable to the Jews, are revealing in that he was a practicing Catholic, not hostile to organized religion, as were Voltaire and Gibbon, but his sympathy for the plight of the Jews retained large reservations about them in their present state. Grégoire believed, as did many others, that centuries of oppression and unfavorable environment were the main reason for Jewish defects, whether physical or spiritual. [The wording has been slightly altered in a few places to enhance readability.]

But the Jews, I shall be told, are incapable of being reformed, because they are absolutely worthless. I reply that we see few of them commit murder, or other enormous crimes ... but their abominable meanness [stinginess] produces base accusations. ... So many laws made against the Jews always suppose in them a natural and indelible worthlessness; but these laws, which are the fruit of hatred or prejudice, have no other foundation but the motive that gives rise to them. The perversity of the Jews is not so inherent in their character as to affect every individual. We see talents and virtues shine forth in them wherever they begin to be treated as men, especially in the territories of the Pope, which have so long been their terrestrial paradise; in Holland, Prussia, and even among us [French]. ... We must then believe these people susceptible of morality. ... Let us cherish morality, but let us not be so unreasonable as to require it of those whom we have compelled to become vicious. Let us reform their education in order to reform their hearts; it has been long observed that they are men as we, and they are men before they are Jews. ...

We allow that it will be difficult to incorporate them into universal society, but between difficulty and impossibility, there is the same difference as between possibility and impossibility. ...

It is maintained that the Jews abound with bad humours; are very much subject to those disorders which indicate that the blood is corrupted, as appears from their formerly being troubled with leprosy, and at present with scurvy, which has so much affinity to it, and with scrophula, bloody-flux, etc. ... It is also contended that the Jews constantly exhale a bad smell. This, indeed, is not a new opinion ... [some maintain] that the cause of this pretended stink, and of their paleness, which is more real, is their occupations (such as that of selling old clothes) and their poverty. Others ascribe these effects to the frequent use of herbs, such as onions and garlic ... and some to the eating of he-goats, while others pretend that the flesh of geese, which they are remarkably fond of, renders them melancholic and livid, as this food abounds with viscous and gross juices.

[More credible is the charge that] ... from a fear of eating blood, the Jews squeeze it almost entirely from their meat, and by these means deprive it of much of its nutritive juice. ... Similarly, the want of a mixture in the breed causes a race to degenerate and lessens the beauty of individuals. ... The Jewish custom of marrying young is prejudicial to both sexes, which it enervates, causing women to be with child prematurely ... weakening the mother and the fruits of her womb. ...

From Mendes-Flohr and Reinharz, [122], pp. 49–53.

DOCUMENT 7   JOHN ADAMS AND AMERICAN PHILO-
SEMITISM

John Adams (1735–1826), the second president of the United States, represents the tendency of American Enlightened thought to be favorable to the Jews, more free of ambiguities than was the case with most Continental thinkers.

In spite of ... Voltaire, I will insist that the Hebrews have done more to civilize men than any other nation. If I were an atheist, and believed in blind eternal fate, I should still believe that fate had ordained that the Jews be the most essential instrument for civilizing the nations. If I were an atheist of any other sect, who believe, or pretend to believe, that all is ordered by chance, I should believe that chance had ordered the Jews to preserve and propagate to all mankind the doctrine of a supreme, intelligent, wise, almighty sovereign of the universe, which I believe to be the essential principle of all morality, and consequently of all civilization. I cannot say that I love the Jews very much, nor the French, nor the English, nor the Romans, nor the Greeks. We must love all nations as well we can, but it is very hard to love most of them. [letter of Feb. 16, 1809]

I have had occasion to be acquainted with several gentleman of your nation, and to transact business with some of them, whom I found to be men of as liberal minds, as much honor, probity, generosity and good breeding, as any I have known in any sect of religion or philosophy. [in a letter to Mordecai M. Noah, July 31, 1818]

How has it happened that millions of fables, tales, legends have been blended with both Jewish and Christian revelation that have made them the most bloody religions that ever existed! [letter of Dec. 27, 1816]

I wish your nation may be admitted to all privileges of citizens in every country of the world. This country has done much. I wish it may do more; and annul every narrow idea in religion, government, and commerce. ... [letter to M. M. Noah, July 1818]

From Gould, [62], pp. 71–2.

DOCUMENT 8   THOMAS JEFFERSON AND THE JEWS

Thomas Jefferson (1743–1826) was in the main known to be friendly to Jews, but he also believed them in need of reform.

The Jews: Their system was Deism, that is, the belief in only one God. But their ideas of him and his attributes were degrading and injurious. ... Their Ethics were not only imperfect but often irreconcilable with the sound dictates of reason and morality, as they respect intercourse with those around us; and repulsive and anti-social, as respecting other nations. They needed reformation, therefore, in an eminent degree. ... [letter to Benjamin Rush, 1803]

Sir: I thank you for the discourse on the consecration of the Synagogue in your city. ... I have read it with pleasure and instruction, having learned from it some valuable facts in Jewish history which I did not know before. Your sect by its sufferings has furnished a remarkable proof of the universal spirit of religious tolerance inherent in every sect, disclaimed by all while feeble, and practiced by all when in power. Our laws have applied the only antidote to this vice, protecting our religious, as they do our civil, rights, by putting all on an equal footing. But more remains to be done, for although we are free by the law, we are not so in practice; public opinion erects itself into an Inquisition. ... [letter to M. M. Noah in 1818]

From Gould, [62], pp. 76–7.

DOCUMENT 9   THE PROFITABLE EXCHANGE OF ARYAN
AND SEMITE (1885)

Thomas Henry Huxley (1825–95) was most famous for his defense of Charles Darwin's theories of natural selection, not for the use of racist inter-pretations of human history. This passage suggests how much 'Aryan' and 'Semite' had entered into the language of the educated classes and that 'Semite' was not understood uniformly in a derogatory sense, nor were Jews widely viewed as racially inferior by those who claimed to be scientific.

It seems to me that the moral and intellectual life of the civilized nations of Europe is the product of that interaction, sometimes in the way of antag-onism, sometimes in that of profitable interchange, of the Semitic and Aryan races, which commenced with the dawn of history, when Greek and Phoenician came into contact, and has been continued by Carthaginian and Roman, by Jew and Gentile, down to the present day.

  Our art (except perhaps music) and our science are the contributions of the Aryan, but the essence of our religion is derived from the Semite. In the eighteenth century, B.C., in the herd of a world of idolatrous polytheists, the

Hebrew prophets put forth a conception of religion which appears to me to be as wonderful an inspiration of genius as the art of Pheidias or the science of Aristotle. ...

The world being what it was, it is to be doubted whether Israel would have preserved intact the pure ore of religion, which the prophets had extracted for the use of mankind as well as for their nation, had the leaders not been zealous, even to the death. ... The struggle of the Jews, under the Maccabean house, against the Seleucidae was as important for mankind as that of the Greeks against the Persians. And, of all the strange ironies of history, perhaps the strangest is that 'Pharisee' is current as a term of reproach among theological descendents of that sect of Nazarenes who, without the martyr spirit of those primitive Puritans, would never have come into existence. They, like their historical successors, our own Puritans, have shared the general fate of the poor wise men who save cities.

From Gould, [62], pp. 163–4.

DOCUMENT 10   'THE JEWS OPPRESSED OR OPPRESSORS?'
(1877)

The famed Russian novelist, Fyodor Dostoevsky (1821–81), is usually counted in the ranks of the anti-Semites in Russia. In his fiction, Jewish characters do not usually play a major role, although his references to them are almost entirely negative, as was the case with many of the rest of Russian writers in the nineteenth century.

True, it is very difficult to learn the forty-century-long history of a people such as the Jews, but ... this much I know, that in the whole world there is certainly no other people who would be complaining as much about their lot. ... One might think that it is not they who are reigning in Europe, who are directing there at least the stock-exchanges, and therefore politics, domestic affairs, the morality of the states. ...

I am fully unable to believe in the screams of the Jews that they are so down-trodden, oppressed, and humiliated. In my opinion, the Russian peasant, and generally the Russian commoner, bears heavier burdens than the Jew. ...

... One thing I do know for sure ... that among our common people there is no preconceived, a priori, blunt religious hatred of the Jews, something along the lines: 'Judas sold out Christ.' Even if one hears it from little children or drunken persons, nevertheless our people as a whole look upon the Jew ... without preconceived hatred. I have been observing this for fifty years. ... [In prison] Jews ... shunned the Russians, they refused to take meals with them, looked upon them with haughtiness (and where – in a prison!) and generally expressed squeamishness and aversion toward the Russian, toward the 'native' people ...

How would it be if in Russia there were not three million Jews but three million Russians, and there were eighty million Jews ... how would they treat them? Would they permit them to acquire equal rights? Would they permit them to worship freely in their midst? Wouldn't they convert them into slaves? Worse than that: Wouldn't they skin them altogether? Wouldn't they slaughter them to the last man, to the point of complete extermination, as they used to do with alien peoples in ancient times? ...

I assure you that in the Russian people there is no preconceived hatred of the Jew, but perhaps there is a dislike of him, and especially in certain localities, maybe a strong dislike. Oh, this cannot be avoided; this exists, but it arises not at all from the fact that he is a Jew, not because of some racial or religious hate, but it comes from other causes of which not the native people but the Jew himself is guilty.

From Mendes-Flohr and Reinharz, [122], pp. 337–8.

DOCUMENT 11   'A WORD ABOUT OUR JEWRY' (1880)

The anti-Jewish sentiments of Heinrich von Treitschke (1834–96) were in some regards more restrained than those of Dostoevsky, but the two men did agree on the basic point that the Jews were responsible for much of the hatred they encountered and that they exaggerated its extent. Both saw the rise of the Jews, Jewish power, and Jewish arrogance as central issues in provoking hatred of them.

Among the symptoms of a great change in mood of the German nation, none appears so strange as the violent movement against the Jews. Until a few months ago ... [anti-Jewish comments were strictly taboo]. About the national shortcomings of the Germans, the French, and all the other nations, everybody could freely say the worse things; but if someone dared to speak in just and moderate terms about some undeniable weakness of the Jewish character, he was immediately branded as a barbarian and religious persecutor by nearly all the newspapers. ...

Today ... antisemitic societies are formed, the 'Jewish Question' is discussed in noisy meetings, a flood of antisemitic pamphlets appears on the market. There is only too much of dirt and brutality in these doings and it is impossible to suppress one's disgust when one notices that some of these incendiary pamphlets obviously come from Jewish pens. ...

But is there really nothing but mob brutality and business envy at the bottom of this noisy activity? Are these outbreaks of a deep, long-suppressed anger only a momentary outburst, as hollow and irrational as the Teutonic antisemitism of 1819? No, the instinct of the masses has in fact clearly recognized a great danger, a serious sore spot in the new German national life. The current expression, 'the German Jewish Question', is more than an empty phrase.

... [O]ur country is invaded year after year by multitudes of assiduous pants-selling youths from the inexhaustible cradle of Poland, whose children and grandchildren are to be the future rulers of Germany's stock exchanges and Germany's press. This immigration grows visibly in numbers and the question becomes more and more serious: How can this alien nation be assimilated? [These Polish Jews] ... are incomparably more alien to the European and especially the German national character [than earlier Jewish immigrants].

What we demand from our Jewish fellow-citizens is simple: that they become Germans, regard themselves simply and justly as Germans, without prejudice to their faith and sacred past, which all of us hold in reverence. We do not want an era of German–Jewish mixed culture to follow after thousands of years of German civilization. It would be a sin to forget that a great number of Jews, baptized and unbaptized, ... have been Germans in the best sense of the word, men in whom we revere the noble and fine traits of the German spirit. At the same time, it cannot be denied that there are numerous and powerful groups among our Jews who definitely do not have the good will to become simply Germans.

It is painful enough to talk about these things. Even conciliatory words are easily misunderstood here. I think, however, that even some of my Jewish friends will admit, with deep regret, that recently a dangerous spirit of arrogance has arisen in Jewish circles and that the influence of Jewry in our national life, which in former times was often beneficial, has recently been harmful. I refer the reader to *The History of the Jews* by Graetz. What a fanatical fury against the 'arch enemy,' Christianity, what a deadly hatred of the purest and most powerful exponents of the German character, from Luther to Goethe, to Fichte! And what hollow, offensive self-glorification! Here it is proved with continuous satirical invective that the nation of Kant was really educated to humanity by the Jews alone, that the language of Lessing and Goethe became sensitive to beauty, spirit, and wit only through Boerne and Heine!

Is there any English Jew who would dare to slander in such a manner the land that guards and protects him? And this stubborn contempt for the German *goyim* is not at all the attitude of a single fanatic. ... [There is a] number of Semitic hustlers among the third-rank talents. And how firmly this bunch of litterateurs hangs together! ...

Even in the most educated [German] circles, among men who would reject with horror any thought of Christian fanaticism or national arrogance, we hear today the cry, as from one mouth, 'the Jews are our misfortune!'

From Mendes-Flohr and Reinharz, [122], pp. 343–4.

DOCUMENT 12   THE JEW AS OPPRESSOR AND EXPLOITER (1920)

The hostility of the writer, G. K. Chesterton (1874–1936), to Jews was less typical of British than Continental intellectuals; he shared with most of them an emphasis on the alleged Jewish exploitation and oppression of non-Jews.

To talk of Jews as always the oppressed and never as the oppressors is simply absurd; it is as if men pleaded for reasonable help for exiled French aristocrats and ruined Irish landlords, and forget that the French and Irish peasants had any wrongs at all! ...

The Syrians and Arabs, and all the agricultural and pastoral populations of Palestine, are, rightly or wrongly, alarmed and angered by the advent of Jews to power, for the perfectly practical and simple reason of the reputation which the Jews have all over the world. ...

Rightly or wrongly, certain people in Palestine fear the coming of the Jews as they fear the coming of locusts; they regard them as parasites that feed on the community by a thousand methods of financial intrigue and exploitation.

There is not the smallest difficulty in stating in plain words what the Arabs fear in the Jews. They fear in exact terms their knowledge, their experience, and their money. ...

The Jewish state will be a success when the Jews in it are ... the dockers and ditchers and porters and hodsmen. ... It is our whole complaint against the Jew that he does not till the soil with the spade. ... If he asks for the spade he must use the spade, and not merely employ the spade in the sense of hiring half a hundred men to use spades. ... (from a newspaper article in 1920)

From Gould, [62], pp. 405–6.

DOCUMENT 13   JEWISH SUCCESS ENGENDERS FEAR IN NON-JEWS

Mark Twain (1835–1910) was widely seen by Jews and others as friendly, but his analysis of tension between Jews and non-Jews pointed, as did that of many anti-Semites, to real issues, not irrational prejudices or religious fantasies; he interestingly emphasized Jewish superiority and honesty.

I feel convinced that the Crucifixion has not much to do with the world's attitude toward the Jew; that the reasons for it are older than that event. ... I am persuaded that in Russia, Austria, and Germany, nine-tenths of the hostility to the Jew comes from the average Christian's inability to compete successfully with the average Jew in business – in either straight business or the questionable sort.

In Berlin, a few years ago, I read a speech which frankly urged the expulsion of Jews from Germany; and the agitator's *reason* was as frank as his proposition. It was this: *that eighty-five percent* of the successful lawyers in Berlin were Jews, and that about the same percentage of the great and lucrative businesses of all sorts in Germany were in the hands of the Jewish race! Isn't it an amazing confession? ... I must insist upon the [importance of] honesty – it is an essential of successful business, taken by and large. Of course, it does not rule out rascals entirely, even among Christians, but it is a good working rule, nonetheless. The speaker's figures may have been inexact, but *the motive of persecution* stands out clear as day. ... [T]he Christian cannot *compete* with the Jew, and ... hence his very bread is in peril. To human beings this is a much more hate-inspiring thing than is any detail connected with religion.

From Gould, [62], p. 266.

DOCUMENT 14   'THE INTERNATIONAL JEW: THE WORLD'S PROBLEM' (1920)

Henry Ford (1863–1947) and Mark Twain agreed in stressing the role of real, concrete issues, but Ford was much more concerned with charges of Jewish conspiracies than was Mark Twain. Hitler wrote in Mein Kampf *(see Doc. 16) that 'it is the Jews who control the stock exchange forces in the American Union. ... Only a single man, Ford, to their fury, still maintains full independence' [p. 639].*

The Jew is again being singled out for critical attention throughout the world. His emergence in the financial, political, and social spheres has been so complete and spectacular since the war that his place, power, purpose in the world are being given a new scrutiny, much of it unfriendly. Persecution is not a new experience for the Jew, but intensive scrutiny of his nature and super-nationality is. ... Nowadays ... the Jew is being placed ... under the microscope of economic observation that the reasons for his power, the reasons for his separateness, the reasons for his suffering may be defined and understood.

In Russia, he is charged with being the source of Bolshevism. ... We in America, hearing the fervid eloquence and perceiving the prophetic ardor of young Jewish apostles of socialism and industrial reform, can calmly estimate how it may be. In Germany, he is charged with being the cause of the Empire's collapse and a very considerable literature has sprung up, bearing with it a mass of circumstantial evidence that gives the thinker pause. In England, he is charged with being the real world ruler, who rules as a supernation over the nations, rules by the power of gold, and who plays nation against nation for his own purposes, remaining discreetly in the background.

The Jew is the world's enigma. Poor in his masses, he yet controls the world's finances. Scattered abroad without country or government, he yet presents a unity of race continuity which no other people has achieved. ...

If the Jew is in control, how did it happen? This is a free country. The Jew comprises only about three percent of the population. ... If the Jew is in control, is it because of his superior ability, or is it because of the inferiority and don't-care attitude of the Gentiles?

... 'To the victor belongs the spoils' is an old saying. And in a sense it is true that if all this power of control has been gained and held by a few men of a long-despised race, then either they are super-men whom it is futile to resist, or they are ordinary men whom the rest of the world has permitted to obtain an undue and unsafe degree of power. Unless the Jews are super-men, the Gentiles will have themselves to blame for what has transpired, and they can look for rectification in a new scrutiny of the situation and a candid examination of the experience of other countries.

From Mendes-Flohr and Reinharz, [122], pp. 512–14.

DOCUMENT 15   A PRUSSIAN GENERAL'S REMARKS ON THE
                          ROLE OF JEWS IN GERMANY

Paul von Hindenburg (1847–1934), Prussian general and war hero of World War I, served as president of the Weimar Republic from 1925 until his death in 1934, when Hitler took over the office of president.

The Imperial military rules and regulations [before 1919] that were discriminatory to the Jews of our country were not drawn up by me. As a subordinate to the high military command, I had to abide by these laws, of course. But let me assure you that I was never in favor of any discriminatory laws against any element of our citizenship. ...

The Jewish people have given to humanity some of its greatest men. Germany is proud to have among its citizens a scholar of the caliber of Prof. Einstein. I do not need to tell you that in Germany your race has a significant share in the development of German culture. ...

Informed as I am of the multiple activities of the Jewish race, familiar with their history and coming in contact with the outstanding representatives of your race, I fully appreciate the part Jews play in Germany and all over the world in the advancement of humanity toward a better world. ...

No, there is no room for intolerance and prejudice, if permanent world peace is to be established. That is why I granted you this interview, in spite of my aversion to talking to the press, in order to make it clear once and for all that democratic Germany will not tolerate any prejudice toward any race or creed. (In an interview granted to Miriam Sterner, in *American Jewish World*, June 29, 1928.)

From Gould, [62], pp. 210–11.

DOCUMENT 16 HITLER DESCRIBES HIS GROWING AWARENESS OF THE JEWISH QUESTION

Adolf Hitler (1889–1945) dictated these remarks, while serving a prison term, to Rudolf Hess, and they were published in 1925 in his book, Mein Kampf *(My Struggle).*

There were few Jews in Linz [the town in which he grew up]. In the course of the centuries their outward appearance had become Europeanized and had taken on a human look. In fact, I even took them for Germans. The absurdity of the idea did not dawn on me because I saw no distinguishing feature but the strange religion. ....

Then I came to Vienna.

... Notwithstanding that Vienna in those days counted nearly two hundred thousand Jews among its two million inhabitants, I did not see them. In the first few weeks my eyes and my senses were not equal to the flood of values and ideas. Not until calm gradually returned and the agitated picture began to clear did I look around me more carefully in my new world, and then among other things I encountered the Jewish Question.

I cannot maintain that the way in which I became acquainted with them struck me as particularly pleasant. For the Jew was still characterized for me by nothing but his religion, and therefore, on grounds of human tolerance, I maintained my rejection of religious attacks in this case as in others. Consequently, the tone, particularly that of the Viennese anti-Semitic press, seemed to me unworthy of the cultural tradition of a great nation. ...

It cost me the greatest inner struggles, and only after months of battle between my reason and my sentiments did my reason begin to emerge victorious. Two years ago, my sentiments had followed my reason, and from then on became its most loyal guardian. ...

Once, as I was strolling through the Inner City, I suddenly encountered an apparition in a black caftan and black hair locks. Is this a Jew? was my first thought. For, to be sure, they had not looked like that in Linz. I observed the man furtively and cautiously, but the longer I stared at this foreign face, scrutinizing feature for feature, the more my first question assumed a new form. Is this a German?

... Wherever I went, I began to see Jews, and the more I saw, the more sharply they became distinguished in my eyes from the rest of humanity. Particularly in the Inner City and districts north of the Danube Canal swarmed a people which even outwardly had lost all resemblance to Germans. ... By their very exterior you could tell that these were no lovers of water, and, to your distress, you often knew it with your eyes closed. Later I often grew sick to my stomach from the smell of these caftan-wearers. Added to this, there was their unclean dress and their generally unheroic appearance.

All of this could scarcely be called very attractive. But it became positively repulsive when, in addition to their physical uncleanliness, you discovered the moral stains on this 'chosen people.' ... Was there ever any form of filth or profligacy, particularly in cultural life, without at least one Jew involved in it? If you cut ... into such an abscess, you found, like a maggot in a rotting body, dazzled by the sudden light – a kike!

From Hitler, [74], pp. 52–7.

DOCUMENT 17   **A PROTEST AGAINST ANTI-SEMITISM**
                    (Jan. 16, 1921)

This protest was published in the New York Times, *Jan. 16, 1921, pp. 30–1, and signed by President Woodrow Wilson, former president William H. Taft, and over a hundred other prominent leaders in religion, politics, business, and education. The organizer of the protest emphasized that 'neither directly nor indirectly did any person of Jewish ancestry or faith, or any Jewish organization, contribute as much as a postage stamp to the cost of the undertaking.'*

The undersigned, citizens of Gentile birth and Christian faith, view with profound regret and disapproval the appearance in this country of what is apparently an organized campaign of antisemitism, conducted in close conformity to and cooperation with similar campaigns in Europe. We regret exceedingly the publication of a number of books, pamphlets, and newspaper articles designed to foster distrust and suspicion of our fellow citizens of Jewish ancestry and faith – distrust of their loyalty and their patriotism.

These publications ... are thus introducing into our national political life a new and dangerous spirit, one that is wholly at variance with our traditions and ideals and subversive of our system of government. American citizenship and American democracy are thus challenged and menaced. ... The logical outcome of the success of such a campaign must necessarily be the division of our citizens along racial and religious lines, and, ultimately, the introduction of religious tests and qualifications to determine citizenship.

The loyalty and patriotism of our fellow citizens of the Jewish faith is equal to that of any part of our people and requires no defense at our hands. From the foundation of this Republic down to the World War, men and women of Jewish ancestry and faith have taken an honorable part in building up this great nation and maintaining its prestige and honor among the nations of the world. There is not the slightest justification, therefore, for a campaign of antisemitism in this country.

Antisemitism is almost invariably associated with lawlessness and with brutality and injustice. It is also invariably found closely intertwined with other sinister forces, particularly those which are corrupt, reactionary, and oppressive.

We believe that it should not be left to men and women of Jewish faith to fight this evil, but that it is in a very special sense the duty of citizens who are not Jews by ancestry or faith. We therefore make earnest protest against this vicious propaganda, and call upon our fellow citizens of Gentile birth and Christian faith to unite their efforts to ours. ... In particular, we call upon all those who are molders of public opinion – the clergy and ministers of all Christian churches, publicists, teachers, editors, and statesmen – to strike at this un-American and un-Christian agitation.

From Mendes-Flohr and Reinharz, [122], p. 514.

GLOSSARY AND CAST OF CHARACTERS

Abraham   biblical character (*c.* 2000) revered as the first patriarch, chosen by God and father of the Hebrew people through Isaac (son) and Jacob (grandson); revered also by Moslems.

Alexander the Great (356–23 BC)   born in Macedonia, tutored by the great philosopher, Aristotle; at a young age he conquered much of the eastern Mediterranean, including most of the great empires of the day; his successors included the Seleucids (from one of his generals, Seleucus), among whom was Antiochus Epiphanes.

Alexander II (1818–81)   Tsar of Russia from 1855 to 1881, known as 'Tsar Liberator,' since he freed the serfs and introduced other wide-ranging reforms; assassinated in 1881, setting off riots against the Jews.

Alexander III (1845–94)   Tsar of Russia from 1881 to 1894, introduced repressive measures after the assassination of his father, including the anti-Jewish May Laws of 1882.

Alexandria   major city in ancient times on the Egyptian coast, founded by Alexander the Great; long a cultural center for both Jews and Greeks, especially famous for its library.

Alliance Israélite Universelle   organization founded in France in 1860 to defend Jewish liberties and provide Jewish education in areas outside France; seen by anti-Semites as a front for international machinations by Jews.

Amalek (Amalekites)   regarded as the arch foe of Israel, one that should be obliterated; the Amalekites attacked the Israelites as they were wandering in the wilderness and remained foes of the Israelites to the time of the Kingdom of David; associated with Haman.

Amos   Jewish prophet, eighth century BC, known for attacking the Israelites of his day for immorality and social injustice.

Antiochus Epiphanes (ruled 175–164 BC)   Syrian Greek (Seleucid) ruler, an ardent Hellenizer whose excesses led to the Hasmonean revolt, background to the festival of Hanukkah.

Bismarck, Otto von (1815–98)   the first Chancellor of the German Empire and architect of German national unification in the 1860s to 1871; dominated European international relations between 1871 and 1890.

Blum, Léon (1872–1950)   prominent leader of the French socialists (SFIO), first Jew to be premier of France, as leader of the Popular Front government in 1936.

Böckel, Otto (1859–1923)   the 'Peasant King,' leader of anti-Semitic peasant movement in Hesseland, Germany.

Bolshevik (Bolshevism)   initially a faction of the Russian Social Democratic Workers' Party ('bolshevik' means 'majoritarian'), finally broke away completely and in 1919 adopted the name 'Communist' after assuming power in Russia in the autumn of 1917; differed from western Marxist or social democratic parties by a stronger emphasis on elitist-dictatorial rule.

Canaan (Canaanites)   the land (and peoples) in ancient times between the Jordan River and the Mediterranean, from Syria to Egypt; conquered by Joshua and the Israelites; special warnings against the 'idolatrous' people of this land and prohibitions in their regard (e.g., intermarriage) became part of Judaism.

Chamberlain, Austen (1863–1937)   British Conservative statesman, held many Cabinet posts and was awarded the Nobel Peace Prize in 1925 for negotiating the Locarno Pact.

Chamberlain, Houston Stewart (1855–1927)   British-born author who spent much of his life in Germany; married the daughter of the composer, Richard Wagner; most famous for his work *Foundations of the Nineteenth Century.*

Cheka   the secret police in Soviet Russia, known to have large numbers of Jews in leading positions; later called the OGPU and GPU. *See also* Dzerzhinsky.

Chmielnicki, Bogdan (1595–1657)   leader of the Cossack uprising in 1648–49 against the Poles; his troops attacked Jews as allies of the Poles, killing thousands.

Christian Social(ism)   term used for a number of movements, notably in Germany and Austria, that tried to reconcile Christian ethics and modern economic systems.

Chrysostom (Saint John) (c. 347–407) Church Father renowned for his eloquence and attacks on Judaism.

Churchill, Winston (1874–1965) British statesman and author, most famous as prime minister during World War II.

Constantine (c. 274–337) Roman Emperor, the first to promote Christianity in the Empire.

Coughlin, Father Charles Edward (1891–1978) Catholic priest whose popular radio shows in the 1930s attacked many targets, including Franklin Delano Roosevelt and the Jews.

Crusades a series of campaigns between the eleventh and fourteenth centuries to recover the Holy Land from the Moslems; the Crusaders often attacked Jewish communities in Europe before departing for Palestine.

Darwin, Charles (1809–82) naturalist and discoverer of natural selection; his major work was *On the Origin of Species by Means of Natural Selection* (1859); the social darwinists claimed to apply his theories to society.

deicide (lit., 'god killing') the Christian doctrine that Jews, in the Crucifixion of Christ, tried to kill God and retained a fanatical hatred of Christ's followers.

Deutscher, Isaac (1907–67) Polish-born author, associated with the Communist movement but broke with Stalin and fled to Britain; wrote biographies of both Stalin and Trotsky.

Dickens, Charles (1812–70) celebrated Victorian author; among his many novels was *Oliver Twist*, with the loathsome Jewish character, Fagin.

Diderot, Denis (1713–84) *philosophe* and critic, most famous as the editor of *Encyclopédie* (1745), a compendium of the most advanced knowledge of the time.

Disraeli, Benjamin (1804–81) British statesman and author, regarded as the founder of the modern Conservative Party.

Dostoevsky, Fyodor (1821–81) Russian novelist, best known for his *Crime and Punishment*.

Dreyfus, Alfred (1859–1935) a French captain falsely accused of delivering military secrets to the Germans; a huge affair developed in France in 1898 over the question of his guilt.

Drumont, Edouard (1844–1917) French journalist, most famous for his anti-Semitism and the role he played in the Dreyfus Affair.

Dual Monarchy formed in 1867, combining Austrian and Hungarian lands under the Habsburg Emperor (Kaiser), Franz Joseph; dissolved in 1919.

Duce Mussolini's title, 'leader' in Italian, comparable to German 'Führer', Hitler's title.

Dühring, Eugen (1833–1921) German economic and social theorist, known for his anti-Semitism and his advocacy of a strong labor movement to control the abuses of capitalism.

Dzerzhinsky, Felix (1877–1926) first head of the Cheka or secret police; spearheaded a reign of terror against the enemies of the Bolshevik regime.

Einstein, Albert (1879–1955) German-born theoretical physicist of Jewish background, one of the most famous scientists of all time.

Eliot, T(homas) S(tearns) (1888–1965) celebrated poet, playwright, and critic; Nobel Prize for Literature in 1948; born in St Louis, MO, but spent most of his life in Great Britain and became a British citizen in 1927; among his most famous works was *The Waste Land* (1922).

Engels, Friedrich (1820–95) German-born socialist, collaborated with Karl Marx in the *Communist Manifesto* (1848), known as the co-founder of the Marxist movement.

Esau biblical figure, brother of Jacob, son of Rebecca and Isaac, considered the archetypical non-Jew, forefather of the Other Nations (*goyim*).

Fagin *See* Dickens, Charles.

Ford, Henry (1863–1947) pioneering American automobile manufacturer, inaugurated a period of anti-Semitic publication in the 1920s.

Freud, Sigmund (1856–1939) psychoanalyst, practicing in Vienna; *The Interpretation of Dreams* (1900) is one of the more famous of his many works, best known for his emphasis on sexuality and the role of the subconscious.

galut Hebrew term for 'exile' or Diaspora, the dispersal of the Jews from their Promised Land. *See* Zionism.

Gentile from Greek and Roman, roughly equivalent to the Hebrew *goy*.

Georgia (Georgian)   area along the Black Sea, briefly independent after the collapse of tsarist Russia, then becoming a Soviet Socialist Republic (Stalin's birth-place; to be distinguished from the American state of Georgia).

Gibbon, Edward (1737–94)   British historian, famous for his work, *The Decline and Fall of the Roman Empire* (5 vols), written between 1776 and 1788.

Gobineau, Count Arthur de (1816–82)   French diplomat and author, known for his work on the role of race – and the dangers of race mixing – in history.

Goethe, Johann Wolfgang von (1749–1832)   Germany's most illustrious poet, author of *Faust*.

Golden Calf   an idol fashioned from the golden jewelry of the Israelites in Moses's absence and worshipped, angering God and nearly ending his covenant with them.

goy (pl. goyim)   Hebrew word for 'nation' (or Other Nations) the equivalent of 'Gentile' or non-Jew.

halakha   traditional Jewish law as contained in the Talmud and post-talmudic literature; Orthodox Jews follow it closely, whereas Reform and Conservative Jews abandon or modify it to varying degrees.

Hanukkah   festival of eight days to commemorate the uprising by the Hasmoneans, under Judah Maccabee; the festival centers around the miracle in the Temple when oil sufficient only for one day lasted for eight.

Herzl, Theodor (1860–1904)   journalist and Zionist leader, born in Budapest, author of *The Jewish State* (1896).

Hitler, Adolf (1889–1945)   leader (Führer) of the National Socialists in Germany; became Chancellor of the Weimar Republic in February 1933 and rapidly established a dictatorship; a powerful demagogue, known for extreme nationalism and anti-Semitism, culminating in the mass murder of Europe's Jews.

Isaac   biblical figure, one of the Patriarchs, son of Abraham, father of Esau and Jacob.

Jacob   biblical figure, son of Isaac and Rebecca, twin brother of Esau, assumed the name 'Israel' and is considered the forefather of the Jews or Israelites.

Joshua biblical figure, appointed by Moses as his successor, commander of the Israelites in their conquest of Canaan.

Junker Prussian aristocracy, played a large role in the military and upper civil service of Prussia and the unified German Reich; many held large estates to the east of the Elbe River.

Koestler, Arthur (1905–83) Hungarian-born Jewish author, most famous for his books *Darkness at Noon* (1940), describing his disillusionment with Communism, and *The Act of Creation* (1964).

Lagarde, Paul de (1827–91) German scholar, known as one of the most important biblical critics and Oriental philologists of the century, as well as a virulent anti-Semite.

Langbehn, Julius (1851–1907) author of the best-selling book, *Rembrandt as Educator* (1890); influential 'German Ideologist' of the 1890s but especially after World War I; strong emphasis on the role of race and blood in human affairs.

Lenin, Vladimir Ilyich (1870–1924) (real name: Ulyanov) founder of the Bolshevik Party and architect of the Bolshevik Revolution in November 1917.

Lessing, Gottfried (1729–81) German philosopher and man of letters, one of the most influential of the German Enlightenment, known especially for his philo-Semitism.

Lindbergh, Charles Augustus (1902–74) American aviator and popular hero, made the first solo non-stop transatlantic flight in 1927; advocate of isolationism in the 1930s; his book *The Spirit of St. Louis* (also the name of his plane) won the Pulitzer Prize in 1953.

Ludendorff, Erich (1865–1937) German general and war hero in World War I, briefly allied with Hitler in the 1920s.

Lueger, Karl (1844–1910) Leader of the Austrian Christian Social Party and mayor of Vienna from 1897 to 1910.

Luther, Martin (1483–1546) German monk who broke with the Catholic Church and translated the Bible into German, consistent with his belief in the priesthood of all believers; known as the founder of the Protestant Reformation.

Maimonides (1135–1204)   a major Jewish scholar and religious author, though highly controversial in his own time; born in Spain and died in Cairo; his most important work was the *Guide for the Perplexed,* which had an important influence on Christian as well as Jewish thinkers.

Manetho (wrote from late fourth to early third century BC)   Egyptian priest and historian; his works are not known in the original but only through references in the writings of later authors.

Mark Twain (1835–1910) (real name: Samuel Longhorne Clemens)   American author whose beloved and enormously influential *Adventures of Huckberry Finn* has been called the first modern American novel.

Marr, Wilhelm (1819–1914)   German journalist, known as the 'Patriarch of Anti-Semitism,' largely because of his best-selling pamphlet, *The Victory of Jews over the Germans* (1879); he had a long and varied career, in his sixties when his pamphlet was published and surviving into his nineties.

Marx, Karl (1818–83)   German-born economist, social theorist, and socialist activist; Marxist parties (usually called 'social democratic') recognizing his theoretical contribution grew up in most of Europe in the late nineteenth century.

matzos   unleavened bread for use in the Passover ceremony.

Mehring, Franz   late nineteenth-century social democrat and biographer of Karl Marx.

Mein Kampf ('My Struggle' in German)   Hitler's account of his life, written while in prison in 1924.

Mendelssohn, Moses (1729–86)   German-Jewish philosopher, leader of the movement for cultural assimilation and modernization of Germany's Jews; life-long friend of Lessing (q.v.).

Moses (13th–14th century BC)   biblical figure, leader of the Hebrew slaves out of Egypt, recipient of the Ten Commandments at Mount Sinai.

Mussolini, Benito (1883–1945)   leader of the fascist movement and dictator (*Duce*) of Italy from 1922 to 1945.

Namier, Sir Lewis Bernstein (1888–1960)   Polish-born British historian, best known for his analysis of the operations of parliament in the mid-eighteenth century.

Napoleon (1769–1821)   Consul (1799) and then Emperor of the French from 1804 to his fall from power in 1814, famous general and law-giver.

Nicholas I (1796–1855)   Tsar of Russia from 1825 to 1855, notorious as a reactionary.

Nicholas II (1868–1918)   Tsar of Russia from 1894 to 1918, when he was put to death by the Bolsheviks.

Nietzsche, Friedrich (1844–1900)   German philosopher, scholar, and essayist; among his many highly regarded and influential works was *Thus Spake Zarathustra* (1888–92); elitist and anti-democratic, he introduced such terms as 'superman' (*Übermensch*), later picked up by the Nazis.

Orthodox   for Jews the term refers to those who resisted the Reform Judaism in the nineteenth century and continued to insist on a strict adherence to traditional practices and beliefs; for Christians the term refers to Eastern Orthodox faith (branches: Greek and Russian), differing from Catholicism most notably in rejecting fidelity to the Pope in Rome.

Pan-Germanism   ideology that forwarded the notion of uniting all German-speakers in Europe into one state, as distinguished from Germans remaining divided in various states. (Other 'pan' movements evolved in the nineteenth and twentieth centuries, such as Pan-Slavism or Pan-Arabism.)

Pharaoh   the god-king of ancient Egypt; Rameses II may have been the pharaoh of the account in the Book of Exodus (13th–14th century BC).

Proudhon, Pierre-Joseph (1809–65)   Prolific and influential French author; his books include *What is Property?* (his answer: theft!) and *War and Peace* (which influenced the great Russian novelist, Tolstoy).

Rathenau, Walther (1862–1922)   German industrialist, intellectual, and statesman; first Jew to serve as foreign minister; assassinated by right-wing fanatics in 1922.

Rebecca (Rebekah)   biblical figure, wife of Isaac, mother of Esau and Jacob.

Renan, Ernst (1823–92)   celebrated and prolific historian of religion; his *Life of Jesus* (1863) was very widely read and influential.

Rothschilds   famous family of bankers and financiers, with branches in nearly every capital of Europe; they were often believed to exercise clandestine power over the destinies of Europe's states.

social darwinism   *See* Darwin, Charles.

socialism, (socialist, social democrat)   a broad movement in the late nineteenth and early twentieth centuries, calling for the abolition of capitalism and class society, to be replaced by planned production and a more equitable distribution of goods and social ownership of the means of production; in 1919 the socialists split into democratic socialist and communist movements.

Spinoza, Baruch (1632–77)   rationalist philosopher born in Amsterdam of Jewish family that had fled Portugal; most famous for his works on optics and astronomy, as well as for his *Tractatus Theologico-Politicus* (1670) and *Ethics* (1677), which arrived at conclusions about biblical religion that outraged both Jews and Christians.

Stoecker, Adolf (1835–1910)   court chaplain to the German Kaiser; began in 1878 a campaign against capitalist wrong-doing and the alleged destructive influence of Jews in German life.

Talmud 'learning' in Hebrew; a comprehensive term for a vast body of commentaries on the Bible and other aspects of Jewish life and laws; there are two versions, the Palestinian (4th century) and Babylonian (5th century).

Treitschke, Heinrich von (1834–96)   celebrated German historian and university professor at Berlin University; liberal and nationalistic as a young man, he became an enthusiastic supporter of Prussia and moved toward glorification of the Prussian state and hostility to its critics, especially Jews.

Trotsky, Leon (1879–1940) (real name: Lev Davidovich Bronstein)   Russian Jewish revolutionary; joined Lenin's Bolshevik Party in 1917, broke with Stalin after Lenin's death and was expelled from the Soviet Union.

Voltaire (1694–1778) (real name: François Marie Arouet)   the most famous of the *philosophes*, a prolific writer, best known for his satirical short story, *Candide* (1759) and the *Philosophical Dictionary* (1764).

Zionism modern Jewish nationalism; extremely diverse in nature and emphasis, but best known as political Zionism, looking to the establishment of a Jewish nation state.

BIBLIOGRAPHY

The relevant literature is so vast that any list is bound to be somewhat arbitrary. The titles listed below include a number of standard works, a sampling of some of the more recent studies, and those that have most influenced me, as well of course as the titles cited in the text. Many of these titles themselves have extensive or otherwise useful bibliographical sections. Particularly worth mention in that regard is Richard S. Levy's *Antisemitism in the Modern World* [106].

1   Adam, U. D., *Judenpolitik im dritten Reich*, Dusseldorf, 1971.
2   Adler, M. (ed.), *Great Books of the Western World*, Chicago, 1952.
3   Alderman, G., *The Jewish Community in British Politics*, Oxford, 1983.
4   Almog, S. (ed.), *Antisemitism through the Ages*, New York, 1988.
5   Almog, S., *Nationalism and Antisemitism in Modern Europe, 1815–1945*, New York, 1990.
6   Angress, W., 'Das deutsche Militär und die Juden im Ersten Weltkrieg', *Militärgeschichtliche Mittelungen*, vol. 19 (1976), 77–146.
7   Aronson, M., 'Geographical and socio-economic factors in the 1881 pogroms in Russia', *The Russian Review*, vol. 39, no. 1 (Jan. 1980), 18–31.
8   Aschheim, S. E., *Brothers and Strangers: The East European Jew in German-Jewish Consciousness*, Madison, Wisc., 1982.
9   Auerbach, J. S., *Rabbis and Lawyers: The Journey from Torah to Constitution*, Bloomington, Ind., 1991.
10   Baron, S. W., *A Social and Religious History of the Jews* (19 vols), New York, 1952–83.
11   Baron, S. W., *Steeled by Adversity: Essays and Addresses on American Jewish Life*, Philadelphia, Penn., 1971.
12   Baron, S. W., *The Russian Jew under Tsars and Soviets*, New York, 1976.
13   Bein, A., *The Jewish Question: Biography of a World Problem*, Rutherford, N.J., 1989.
14   Beller, S., *Vienna and the Jews, 1867–1938*, Cambridge, Eng., 1989.

15   Ben-Sasson, H. H. (ed.), *A History of the Jewish People*, Cambridge, Mass., 1976.

16   Berg, S., *Lindbergh*, New York, 1998.

17   Berger, D. (ed.), *The Legacy of Jewish Migration: 1881 and its Impact*, New York, 1983.

18   Berlin, I., *Against the Current: Essays in the History of Ideas*, London, 1979.

19   Bermant, C., *The Cousinhood*, London, 1971.

20   Best, G. D., *To Free a People: American Jewish Leaders and the Jewish Problem in Eastern Europe, 1890–1914*, Westport, Conn., 1982.

21   Biale, D., *Power and Powerlessness in Jewish History*, New York, 1986.

22   Blackbourn, D. and Eley, G., *The Peculiarities of German History*, Oxford, 1984.

23   Borden, M., *Jews, Turks, and Infidels*, Chapel Hill, N.C., 1984.

24   Boyer, J. W., *Political Radicalism in Late Imperial Vienna*, Chicago, Ill., 1981.

25   Bredin, J.–D., *The Affair: The Case of Alfred Dreyfus*, New York, 1986.

26   Bristow, E. J., *Prostitution and Prejudice: The Jewish Fight against White Slavery, 1870–1939*, New York, 1983.

27   Burns, M., *Rural Society and French Politics: Boulangism and the Dreyfus Affair, 1886–1900*, Princeton, N.J., 1986.

28   Cannistraro, P. V. and Sullivan, B. R., *Il Duce's Other Woman: The Untold Story of Margherita Sarfatti*, New York, 1993.

29   Cantor, Norman, *The Sacred Chain: The History of the Jews*, New York, 1994.

30   Carlebach, J., *Karl Marx and the Radical Critique of Judaism*, London, 1978.

31   Carsten, F. L., *The Rise of Fascism*, Berkeley, Calif., 1980.

32   Chazan, R., *Medieval Stereotypes and Modern Antisemitism*, Berkeley, Calif., 1997.

33   Clare, G., *The Last Waltz in Vienna: The Rise and Fall of a Family, 1842–1942*, New York, 1981.

34   Cohen, J., *The Friars and the Jews: Evolution of Medieval Anti-Judaism*, Ithaca, N.Y., 1982.

35   Cohen, M. J., *Churchill and the Jews*, Totowa, N.J., 1985.

36   Cuddihy, J. M., *The Ordeal of Civility: Freud, Marx, Lévy-Strauss, and the Jewish Struggle with Modernity*, New York, 1974.

37   Cuddihy, J. M., 'The Elephant and the Angels; or, The Incivil Irritatingness of Jewish Theodicy', in N. Bellah, and E. Greenspahn, (eds), *Uncivil Religion*, New York, 1987.

38   De Felice, R., *Storia degli ebrei italiani sotto il fascismo*, Milan, 1961.

39   Dershowitz, A., *Chutzpah*, Boston, Mass., 1991.

40   Deutscher, I., *Trotsky: The Prophet Armed: Trotsky, 1879–1921*, Oxford, 1954.

41 Deutscher, I., *The Non-Jewish Jew and Other Essays*, London, 1968.
42 Dinnerstein, L. (ed.), *Anti-Semitism in the United States*, New York, 1971.
43 Dinnerstein, L., *Uneasy at Home*, New York, 1987.
44 Dinnerstein, L., *Anti-Semitism in America*, Oxford, 1994.
45 Edelstein, A., *An Unacknowledged Harmony: Philosemitism and the Survival of European Jewry*, Westport, Conn., 1982.
46 Eley, G., *Reshaping the German Right: Radical Nationalism and Political Change after Bismarck*, New Haven, Conn., 1980.
47 Evans, W. M., 'From the Land of Canaan to the Land of Guinea: The Strange Odyssey of the Sons of Ham', *American Historical Review*, vol. 85, no. 1 (Feb. 1980), 15–42.
48 Fein, L., *Where Are We? The Inner Life of American Jews*, New York, 1988.
49 Field, G., *Evangelist of Race: The Germanic Vision of Houston Stewart Chamberlain*, New York, 1980.
50 Fox, R. L., *The Unauthorized Version: Truth and Fiction in the Bible*, New York, 1992.
51 Frankel, J., *Prophecy and Politics: Socialism, Nationalism, and the Russian Jews, 1862–1917*, Cambridge, Eng., 1981.
52 Friedlander, S., *Nazi Germany and the Jews*, New York, 1997.
53 Friedman, R. E., *Who Wrote the Bible?*, New York, 1987.
54 Gager, J. G., *The Origins of Anti-Semitism: Attitudes toward Judaism in Pagan and Christian Antiquity*, Oxford, 1985.
55 Gay, P., *The Enlightenment*, New York, 1966.
56 Gay, P., *Freud, Jews, and Other Germans*, Oxford, 1978.
57 Geehr, R. S., *Karl Lueger: Mayor of Fin de Siècle Vienna*, Detroit, Mich., 1990.
58 Gerber, D. (ed.), *Anti-Semitism in American History*, Chicago and Urbana, Ill., 1986.
59 Gilbert, M., *Jewish Historical Atlas*, New York, 1976.
60 Ginsberg, B., *The Fatal Embrace: Jews and the State*, Chicago, 1993.
61 Gordon, S., *Hitler, Germans, and the 'Jewish Question'*, Princeton, N.J., 1984.
62 Gould, A., *What Did They Think of the Jews?*, Northvale, N.J., 1991.
63 Gould, S. J., *The Mismeasure of Man*, New York, 1981.
64 Grant, M., *The Jews in the Ancient World*, New York, 1984.
65 Griffiths, R., *Fellow Travellers of the Right: British Enthusiasts for Nazi Germany*, London, 1980.
66 Grose, P., *Israel in the Mind of America*, New York, 1984.
67 Hagen, W., *Germans, Poles, and Jews: The Nationality Conflict in East Prussia, 1772–1914*, Chicago, Ill., 1980.
68 Hanfstaengl, E., *Unheard Witness*, New York, 1957.
69 Hertzberg, A., *The French Enlightenment and the Jews: The Origins of Modern Anti-Semitism*, New York, 1968.

70   Hertzberg, A., *The Jews in America: Four Centuries of an Uneasy Encounter*, New York, 1989.

71   Hertzberg, A., *The Jews: The Essence and Character of a People*, San Francisco, Calif., 1998.

72   Higham, J., *Send These to Me: Immigrants in Urban America*, rev. edn, Baltimore, Md., 1984.

73   Himmelfarb, M., 'No Hitler, No Holocaust', *Commentary*, vol. 77, no. 3, (March 1984), 37–43.

74   Hitler, A., *Mein Kampf*, New York, 1971.

75   Hitler, A., *Hitler's Table Talk, 1941–44: His Private Conversations*, London, 1973.

76   Holmes, C., *Anti-Semitism in British Society, 1876–1939*, New York, 1979.

77   Hood, J., *Aquinas and the Jews*, Philadelphia, Penn., 1995.

78   Howe, I., *World of Our Fathers*, New York, 1976.

79   Humer, S. (ed.), *Lenin on the Jewish Question*, New York, 1974.

80   Hyman, P., *From Dreyfus to Vichy: The Remaking of French Jewry, 1906–1939*, New York, 1979.

81   Israel, J. I., *European Jewry in the Age of Mercantilism*, Oxford, 1986.

82   Johnson, P., *A History of the Jews*, New York, 1987.

83   Katz, J., *Exclusiveness and Tolerance: Studies in Jewish–Gentile Relations in Medieval and Modern Times*, Oxford, 1961.

84   Katz, J., *Out of the Ghetto: The Social Background of Jewish Emancipation, 1770–1870*, Cambridge, Mass., 1973.

85   Katz, J., *From Prejudice to Destruction*, Cambridge, Mass., 1981.

86   Katz, J., 'Misreadings of Anti-Semitism', *Commentary*, vol. 76, no. 1, (July 1983), 39–44.

87   Katz, J., *The Darker Side of Genius: Richard Wagner's Anti-Semitism*, Hanover, N. H., 1986.

88   Kaufman, W., *The Portable Nietzsche*, New York, 1968.

89   Kennedy, P. and Nicholls, A. (eds), *Nationalist and Racialist Movements in Britain and Germany before 1914*, London, 1981.

90   Kershaw, I., *The 'Hitler Myth': Image and Reality in the Third Reich*, Oxford, 1989.

91   Kershaw, I., *Hitler, 1889–1936: Hubris*, New York, 1999.

92   Kleeblatt, N. L., *The Dreyfus Affair: Art, Truth, and Justice*, Berkeley, Calif., 1987.

93   Koestler, A., *In the Trail of the Dinosaur and Other Essays*, New York, 1955.

94   Kolber, F., *Napoleon and the Jews*, New York, 1977.

95   Lamberti, M., *Jewish Activism in Imperial Germany*, New Haven, Conn., 1982.

96   Lambroza, S., 'The Tsarist Government and the Pogroms of 1903–06', *Modern Judaism*, vol. 7, no. 3 (Oct. 1987), 287–96.

97   Lambroza, S. and Klier, J., *Pogroms: Anti-Jewish Violence in Modern Russian History*, Cambridge, Eng., 1992.

98   Lane, B. M. and Rupp, L. J. (eds), *Nazi Ideology before 1933, a Documentation*, London, 1978.

99   Langer, L., *Admitting the Holocaust*, Oxford, 1995.

100 Langmuir, G., *Toward a Definition of Antisemitism*, Berkeley, Calif., 1990.

101 Lazare, B., *Antisemitism: Its History and Causes*, Lincoln, Neb., 1995.

102 Lebzelter, G., *Political Antisemitism in England, 1918–1939*, London, 1978.

103 Lee, A., *Henry Ford and the Jews*, New York, 1980.

104 Lewis, B., *Semites and Anti-Semites*, New York, 1986.

105 Levy, R. S., *The Downfall of the Anti-Semitic Parties in Imperial Germany*, New Haven, Conn., 1975.

106 Levy, R. S., *Antisemitism in the Modern World: An Anthology of Texts*, Lexington, Mass., 1991.

107 Lindemann, A. S., *The Jew Accused: Three Anti-Semitic Affairs, Dreyfus, Beilis, Frank, 1894–1915*, Cambridge, Eng., 1991, ppr. 1993.

108 Lindemann, A. S., *Esau's Tears: Modern Anti-Semitism and the Rise of the Jews*, Cambridge, Eng., 1997.

109 Low, A. D., *Jews in the Eyes of Germans: From the Enlightenment to Imperial Germany*, Philadelphia, Penn., 1979.

110 Lukacs, J., *The Hitler of History*, New York, 1998.

111 MacDonald, K., *A People Shall Dwell Alone: Judaism as a Group Evolutionary Strategy*, Westport, Conn., 1994.

112 MacDonald, K., *Culture of Critique: An Evolutionary Analysis of Jewish Involvement in Twentieth Century Intellectual and Political Movements*, Westport, Conn., 1998.

113 MacDonald, K., *Separation and its Discontents: Toward an Evolutionary Theory of Anti-Semitism*, Westport, Conn., 1998.

114 Malino, F. and Wasserman, B. (eds), *The Jews of Modern France*, Hanover, N.H., 1985.

115 Marr, W., *Der Sieg des Judenthums über das Germanenthum*, Bern, 1879.

116 Marrus, M., *The Politics of Assimilation: A Study of the Jewish Community at the Time of the Dreyfus Affair*, Oxford, 1971.

117 Maser, W., *Hitler: Legend, Myth, and Reality*, New York, 1973.

118 Massing, P., *Rehearsal for Destruction*, New York, 1967.

119 McCagg, W. O., Jr., *Jewish Nobles and Geniuses in Modern Hungary*, New York, 1972.

120 McCagg, W. O., Jr., *A History of Habsburg Jews, 1670–1918*, Bloomington, Ind., 1989.

121 Mendelsohn, E., *Class Struggles in the Pale: The Formative Years of the Jewish Workers' Movement in Tsarist Russia*, Cambridge, Eng., 1970.

122 Mendes-Flohr, P. and Reinharz, J. (eds), *The Jew in the Modern World: A Documentary History*, 2nd edn, Oxford, 1995.

123   Meyer, M., *Ideas of Jewish History*, New York, 1971.

124   Michaelis, M., *Mussolini and the Jews, 1922–1945*, Oxford, 1978.

125   Mosse, G., *Toward the Final Solution: A History of European Racism*, New York, 1980.

126   Mosse, G., *German Jews beyond Judaism*, Bloomington, Ind., 1985.

127   Mosse, W. E. (ed.), *Deutsches Judentum in Krieg und Revolution*, Tübingen, 1971.

128   Mosse, W. E., *Jews in the German Economy: The German–Jewish Elite, 1820–1930*, Oxford, 1987.

129   Nadler, Steven, *Spinoza, a Life*, Cambridge, Eng., 1999.

130   Nedava, J., *Trotsky and the Jews*, Philadelphia, Penn., 1971.

131   Nord, P. G., *Paris Shopkeepers and the Politics of Resentment*, Princeton, N.J., 1986.

132   Oldson, W. O., *A Providential Anti-Semitism: Nationalism and Polity in Nineteenth Century Romania*, Philadelphia, Penn., 1991.

133   Oxaal, I. (ed.), *Jews, Antisemitism, and Culture in Vienna*, London and New York, 1987.

134   Patai, R., *The Jewish Mind*, New York, 1977.

135   Pawel, E., *The Labyrinth of Exile: A Life of Theodor Herzl*, New York, 1989.

136   Pipes, R., *The Russian Revolution*, New York, 1991.

137   Poliakov, L., *History of Anti-Semitism* (4 vols), New York, 1965–86.

138   Pulzer, P. G. J., *The Rise of Political Anti-Semitism in Germany and Austria*, New York, 1964.

139   Rauschning, H., *Voice of Destruction*, New York, 1940.

140   Reinharz, J., *Fatherland or Promised Land: The Dilemma of the German Jew, 1893–1914*, Ann Arbor, Mich., 1975.

141   Rezzori, G. von, *Memoirs of an Anti-Semite*, New York, 1981.

142   Rogger, H., *Jewish Politics and Right-wing Politics in Imperial Russia*, Berkeley, Calif., 1986.

143   Rogger, H., *Russia in the Age of Modernization and Revolution, 1881–1917*, New York, 1983.

144   Rose, P. L., *German Question/Jewish Question: Revolutionary Antisemitism from Kant to Wagner*, Princeton, N.J., 1992.

145   Rosenbaum, R., *Explaining Hitler*, New York, 1998.

146   Rosenblit, M. L., *The Jews of Vienna, 1867–1914: Assimilation and Identity*, New York, 1984.

147   Rubinstein, W. D., *A History of the Jews in the English-speaking World: Great Britain*, New York, 1996.

148   Rubinstein, W. D., *The Left, the Right, and the Jews*, London, 1982.

149   Rubinstein, W. D. and Rubinstein, H., *Philosemitism*, London, 1999.

150   Ruether, R., *Faith and Fratricide: The Theological Roots of Anti-Semitism*, New York, 1974.

151   Samuel, M., *Blood Accusation*, New York, 1966.

152   Sandmel, S., *Anti-Semitism in the New Testament*, Philadelphia, Penn., 1978.

153 Sarna, J. D. (ed.), *The American Jewish Experience*, New York, 1986.
154 Schäfer, P., *Judeophobia: Attitudes toward the Jews in the Ancient World*, Cambridge, Mass., 1997.
155 Schauss, H., *The Jewish Holidays: A History and Observance*, New York, 1938.
156 Schorsch, I., *Jewish Reactions to German Anti-Semitism*, New York, 1972.
157 Schorske, C. E., *Fin-de-Siècle Vienna, Politics and Culture*, New York, 1981.
158 Segrè, D. A., *Memoirs of a Fortunate Jew: An Italian Story*, Bethesda, Md., 1987.
159 Shahak, I., *Jewish History, Jewish Religion: The Weight of a Thousand Years*, Boulder, Col. and London, 1994.
160 Sholokov, M., *And Quiet Flows the Don*, Moscow, 1968 [first Russian edn, 1928].
161 Silberman, C. E., *A Certain People: American Jews and Their Lives Today*, New York, 1985.
162 Silberner, E., *Sozialisten zur Judenfrage*, Berlin, 1962.
163 Singer, I., *Russia at the Bar of the American People*, New York, 1904.
164 Singer, I. B., 'Yiddish: The Language of Exile', in D. Villiers, (ed.), *Next Year in Jerusalem*, London, 1976,
165 Smith, P., *Disraeli, a Brief Life*, Cambridge, Eng., 1996, ppr. 1999.
166 Speer, A., *Inside the Third Reich*, New York, 1970.
167 Stanislawski, N., *Tsar Nicholas I and the Jews*, Philadelphia, Penn., 1983.
168 Steinberg, S., *The Ethnic Myth: Race, Ethnicity, and Class in America*, New York, 1981.
169 Stember, C. H. (ed.), *Jews in the Mind of America*, New York, 1966.
170 Stern, F., *The Politics of Cultural Despair: A Study in the Rise of the Germanic Ideology*, New York, 1974.
171 Stern, F., *Gold and Iron: Bismarck, Bleichröder, and the Building of the German Empire*, New York, 1979.
172 Stern, M., *Greek and Latin Authors on Jews and Judaism* (3 vols), Jerusalem, 1974–84.
173 Stille, A., *Benevolence and Betrayal: Five Italian Jewish Families under Fascism*, New York, 1991.
174 Tal, U., *Christians and Jews in Germany: Religion, Politics, and Ideology, 1870–1914*, Ithaca, N.Y., 1975.
175 Toland, J., *Adolf Hitler*, New York, 1976.
176 Trachtenberg, J., *The Devil and the Jews: The Medieval Conception of the Jew and its Relation to Modern Anti-Semitism*, New Haven, Conn., 1943.
177 Traverso, E., *The Jews of Germany: From the 'Judeo-German Symbiosis' to the Memory of Auschwitz*, Lincoln, Nebr., 1995.
178 Twain, M., *Concerning the Jews*, Philadelphia, Penn., 1985 [from March 1898 issue of *Harper's New Monthly Magazine*].

179 Villiers, D. (ed.), *Next Year in Jerusalem*, London, 1976.

180 Whiteside, A., *The Socialism of Fools: Georg Ritter von Schönerer and Austrian Pan-Germanism*, Berkeley, Calif., 1975.

181 Wilken, R. L., *John Chrysostom and the Jews*, Berkeley, Calif., 1983.

182 Wilken, R. L. and Meeks, W. A., *Jews and Christians in Antioch in the First Four Centuries of the Common Era*, Missoula, Mont., 1978.

183 Wilson, S., *Ideology and Experience: Anti-Semitism in France at the Time of the Dreyfus Affair*, East Brunswick, N.J., 1982.

184 Wistrich, R., *Revolutionary Jews from Marx to Trotsky*, New York, 1976.

185 Wistrich, R., *Socialism and the Jews: The Dialectics of Emancipation in Germany and Austria-Hungary*, East Brunswick, N.J., 1984.

186 Wistrich, R., *Antisemitism, The Longest Hatred*, New York, 1991.

187 Wolf, W., *Essays in Jewish History*, London, 1911.

188 Zimmermann, M., *Wilhelm Marr, the Patriarch of Anti-Semitism*, Oxford, 1986.

189 Zipperstein, S., *The Jews of Odessa: A Cultural History, 1794–1881*, Stanford, Calif., 1985.

INDEX